Bullseye

Bullseye

Lannah Sawers-Diggins

Library of Congress Control Number:		2010909898
ISBN:	Hardcover	978-1-4535-2731-3
	Softcover	978-1-4535-2730-6
	Ebook	978-1-4535-1843-4

To order additional copies of this book, contact:
Xlibris Corporation
1-888-795-4274
www.Xlibris.com
Orders@Xlibris.com
81828

DEDICATED TO

VICTIMS OF BULLYING

THE WORLD OVER

CONTENTS

ABOUT THIS BOOK
AND
INTRODUCTION

Bully . . . described in the Concise English Dictionary:

> "a browbeating person, esp someone who is habitually cruel to other weaker people;

> "intimidate with persistently aggressive or violent behaviour, or by using threats of violence;"

These two descriptions are certainly true, but to the victims who have so generously submitted their stories for inclusion in this book . . . they would barely be adequate. I have been one such victim. But my tale of woe is NOTHING compared with the humiliation, embarrassment, degradation and so much more that many of the people featured in this book have suffered, many still suffering.

The suggestion of writing a book about bullying was put to me some years ago . . . I cannot actually recall who did suggest it, or when, but it certainly planted a seed in my mind. Research through those years has suggested that many have written books before me, but no-one seems to have actually devoted a book almost entirely to stories of victims . . . this was my goal. In communicating with these and other victims, both current and past, I found that they all appeared to have the same message . . . just how therapeutic it was to be able to . . . just talk about it . . . get it off their chests. Of course, there are always the exceptions. Sadly, one particular victim has been so badly scarred that he found it too difficult to write his experiences at all. And writing their stories will never change the fact that these people have been bullied. Many have had counselling, many have not . . . many are still undergoing this. Some cases are far more serious than others . . . some have undergone the court process . . . others are still going through this . . .

The stories within these pages vary hugely . . . from supposedly minor cases through to some which are far some serious. But irrespective of the severity of them, the effects on the victims have been horrendous. Many have made my blood boil.

Doing this has given me a very small idea of just how mammoth this problem is and that it is EVERYWHERE. No-one is immune, nor is any institution, any situation. It takes place at any age, any gender, any faith, anywhere, any time.

Many of the victims were bullied in their teens and/or childhood, and some of these people were raised in the years prior to bullying being recognized and/or acknowledged. For some victims it is past tense, for others a very current and continuing nightmare. Some stories have come from various work places. There are even a couple written by people who have been bullied and have been bullies themselves.

What has disturbed and infuriated me throughout (and believe me, I would NOT have wanted to have my blood pressure nor stress levels taken while doing this), something that does appear to be a common thread, particularly with the stories taken from schools . . . in seeking help, justice and compensation through the appropriate channels, the education and legal systems, in almost every case it appears that that the perpetrator/s is/are the ones who have been supported . . . NOT the victims. Most if not all schools maintain that they have a 'bullying policy' in place . . . but given all that is covered in these stories, and some of the outcomes, I do have to question . . . just how effective are these policies and who are they aiming to help????

In one particular case, the victim lost her father, which was tragic enough in itself, but then . . . from what I can see, she was bullied . . . partly for this reason? Losing her father????? WHY? What is the MENTALITY of bullies????

A few of these histories are quite long and, as previously mentioned, some victims continue their fight for compensation and/or justice. I have and do feel so much for the parents, families of the victims and for the victims themselves. Overall from what I have learned, the attitudes of the schools leave me cold. I am not saying that this applies in all cases world wide . . . goodness knows, those in the following pages are only the smallest drop in the ocean compared with the amount of bullying that continues 24/7. But from what I have read through these and dozens of other cases as well . . . sadly that does appear to be true of many schools.

Please bear in mind as you read through that all these cases are direct quotes from victims or a loved one and all have been reproduced with the original spelling, grammar, punctuation etc in place. All case histories have been reproduced as closely as possible to the original texts written by the victims. However, all names of both humans and institutions, towns etc have been changed to protect the innocent.

I know bullying is a widespread and horrible problem and sadly, seems to be increasing and it is everywhere. When I first decided to write this book, I was mainly using it as a therapeutic tool for my own experiences. But then, as mentioned, others heard about this and contacted me . . . and I received a lot of response from some advertising I did . . . and thus my book was born.

I have no idea who will read this publication, and I will not say I hope you enjoy it . . . unlike most publications, that is not the purpose of this book. But I really hope that reading it does do some good, somewhere in this world we live in, to make life more bearable for the victims of bullying.

Lannah Sawers-Diggins

Lannah Sawers-Diggins was born in 1955 in Adelaide, capital of South Australia. She enjoyed a wonderful and quite different childhood on the family sheep station of that state. Her primary education was provided by correspondence school and School of the Air. At eleven years of age, she followed her brothers to different boarding schools in Adelaide. Life at school in those days was completely different to the "home-away-from-home" that boarders enjoy today.

After leaving school in 1972 Lannah went on to hold various positions in Adelaide, before joining the Bank of Adelaide. During her years here she started travelling to interstate branches on "trouble shooting" trips. This gained her a taste of life away from Adelaide—she was never to return to live.

Foreign lands beckoned and Lannah headed to England where she lived, worked and travelled for eleven months. Returning to Australia, she settled in Perth and six months later met and married her husband, Stuart. After a couple of years their eldest daughter, Robyn, was born followed by Fiona and then a job transfer saw Stuart relocate his family across the nation to Sydney. Lannah was heavily involved in all aspects of the girls' early and primary schooling, through their different schools in and around Sydney, before finally returning to Perth to live.

A love of writing and drawing has woven itself through Lannah's life. Once both girls were safely esconced in secondary school, Lannah experimented in various interests and part time positions, before finally settling into her current position with a small, private family run publishing business. Naturally this has provided an insight into the publishing industry, so, along with that love of writing, an avenue was paved to finally immerse herself in this passion and produce two works of utmost personal importance. Firstly, the completed compilation of her late father, Brian Sawers', memories and experiences when settling into life in outback

Australia (*"The Sawers From Pitcairn"*). Secondly, this book . . . a collection of stories recounting the experiences of some thirty six victims and some perpetrators of bullying, a potentially physically and physchologically harmful crime (though unrecognized by law) against anyone of any age, gender or background, that can and *does* take place at any time and in any place.

ACKNOWLEDGEMENTS

First and foremost, a huge thanks to all those victims of bullying who have been wonderful enough to allow me to include your case histories in these pages. I just hope that by writing your experiences down, might have provided you all some sort of relief and release. It will never erase the fact that you have been victims of bullying, but I sincerely hope that this has helped, even if only very slightly. Some of you have already mentioned how therapeutic it was, which is absolutely wonderful, and I really hope that feeling at least applies to all of you. Thank you.

A huge thanks to Philip Sarthou and Ronald Reese for your guidance and endless patience with me during the publication of this book and generally to the wonderful team at Xlibris. Thank you all.

A special thanks to Rebecca Trinca for so generously allowing me to use her superb art for the cover of this book. Thanks Rebecca.

My heartfelt thanks to my wonderful husband, Stuart, two lovely daughters, Robyn and Fiona, and Tristan, for your unwavering belief in me, your love and support and just . . . for being there and for being you. Also to Whiskey and Guacamole . . . I love you all.

The following is a short piece based on a bullying experience the author had in her youth . . . written by a 31 year old woman remembering how she tried to make sense of it all in the world of a 10 year old child.

FALLING STAR

A brilliant star appears in the sky above
With each act of compassionate and unselfish love
When that love has accomplished what it intended to do
The star falls from the sky, especially for you
To fulfil a wish you've held in your heart
As a gift for playing an important part
In transforming a wrong into a right
And showing others through darkness to look for the light.

"Tim" was a young boy, surrounded by friends
Who was popular and kept up with all the new trends
He was concerned for a classmate and couldn't condone
How this stranger was constantly left all alone
It was obvious he was timid and always felt shy
And was regularly bullied until he would cry
Those responsible for the torment were "Tim's" mates
But he didn't have the courage to stop all the hate
Consumed with guilt, he chose to look the other way
Scared of being the new target the following day.

The lunchtime bell rang and when walking outside
The stranger was pushed, again bruising his pride
"Tim" couldn't let this continue another second more
So he knelt down and helped him up from the floor
The stranger was stunned and so were "Tim's" friends
As he shouted, **"From now on this is going to end!"**
He apologised to the stranger for all he'd been through
And firmly asked the others to do the same too
Reluctantly they said "**sorry**" and went on their way
Before asking "Tim" if he was coming to play
He refused because he was determined to show
That the stranger was a new friend he was getting to know.

That night in the heavens a bright star appeared
Because "Tim" helped another and conquered his fear
As a reward for his noble accomplishment
A wish on a falling star would soon be sent.

Next time you are gazing at the night sky
Look up at those stars and think about why
If a good deed is measured by one of those lights
Then with the billions up there, our future looks bright
Behind this story, the meaning is true
Showing love is up to me and to you.'

THE END

The mother of one of the victims provided me with her daughter's story, and has also been good enough to provide the technique they used to help the victim strengthen her self esteem. While the family concerned has requested that the story itself not be printed, they have offered the following suggestions for the benefit of other victims/families of.

My sincere thanks to these people for this.

'The best way for us with my daughter was to help strengthen her self esteem.

'(After the incident) I then spent time with her, briefly as follows:

- who is the nicest and best student in the school? She decided the female school captain we'll call Mia.
- what would Mia say if people said such things to her? They wouldn't.
- can you work out what it is about Mia that stops them? lots of answers here, she's nice, she's brilliant, teachers talk to her all the time, she's lived here all her life and people know her and her family (we had only been in town for a few months)
- how would you feel if you were in Mia's situation? this took quite a while to build a picture.
- can you imagine yourself wearing a cloak of "Mia feelings"?
- so when you walk into class, or playground, or a group of students, take a deep breath and wrap yourself in your "Mia feelings cloak", and keep thinking of how Mia would respond if anyone treated her that way.

'Of course it was not that simple, but this technique was a help. At the end of the year classes were re-sorted, and my daughter found herself in a much better group. But she never regained the confidence to speak out, and her marks went down to strictly average, because she could not bear the thought of attracting any attention.

'After year ten we chose to send her to boarding school . . . her brothers had gone as where we had lived previously, there was no school past year 10 . . . she is still friends with the great girls she met there, (she's 26 now, and two of these friends will be her bridesmaids soon, and there are a half a dozen more attending the wedding) and her marks improved beautifully and continued to do so, every year including University.

'I think I mention the lasting friendships to show she was not a difficult person who would always be targeted!!!'

CASE ONE

'I feel I,m quite a strong person in character, I make freinds quite easily but don,t get the closeness, as over the years I have been hurt and trying to be too friendly, it does,nt work for me. I have been fortunate in my life that I have had three very close freinds, whom I can see day to day or not for weeks and we can still pick up where we left off.

'So leading up to meeting the person for the first time, it was in a bar, where my now husband worked, he use to work in the bar and socialise on his days off, on this occasion I went with him and met for the first time this person. My first impression was that she was foul mouthed and swore a lot, I am not a prude in any way, but having not being brought up in using bad language, I didnt want to be in it now, I must say I'm no inocent, but it,s my choice not to be in this enviroment. And although my now husband was freinds with her and her husband then, I did,nt feel we had anything in common. I hope not to sound snobby, and I hope there are some people out there who would understand how I feel?

'Life moved on, we got married, moved house and I moved jobs to be nearer our new home. One of the first people I saw in my new job was this woman. And I was right to feel that we had nothing in common. She was a Bench leader that consisted of being a supervisor to four women, I was learning the job and at that time did,nt have much to do with her, We were freindly enough to each other but that,s as far as it went, and that suited me.

'In the meantime as time passed, there were redundances, it was,nt a case of last in first out, they did it on attendance, lateness, ect, and one to go was the woman. It was a painfull day as a lot of freinds left, and it unsettled the rest of us that stayed. But we all plodded on, I eventually became a head of Bench and for a while life plodded on, I had a good group of women, or thought I had? Buisness picked up, we got a lot busyer, and the women that had been made redundant were offered their jobs back. And who was to come through the door was the said woman, but I thought that,s OK, as long as she was,nt on my bench I was happy. I don,t know what it was between us, whether she thought I was a snob? Or whether she knew how i felt about her, Basicly I think she was a kind person, but we just did,nt fuse.

'More time passed and we were all taking our holidays, as I returned from mine my biggest nightmare was facing me, the said woman was on my bench and I did,nt have a word to say about it, at first it wasn't too bad but over time the swearing and bad language continued, her attitude towards any one in managment including me was awful, why she came back I will never know, I beleive basicly she was an unhappy person and liked to bring everyone down with her, some days it was,nt what she said but what she did,nt say, the bosses seemed to be very wary of her. She had no respect for them and very little for herself. basicly unhappy but her mouth and attitude let her down everytime. She would refuse to do certain jobs and this rubbed off on the other women on the bench, it was better being in her club than thinking for themselves, it became intollerable, and I had person problems of my own, and not feeling up to par, I became with drawn, hardly spoke all day, hated the thought of going to work, it was a real struggle to cope with. And all the time she would sit in the tea breaks as though butter would,nt melt, and popular because she had the loudest mouth against the managment, and women use to hang onto her every word. I can,t say I hated her, but it came very close. So one day I had had a bad day and blew up, she retaliated and a woman on the bench that I thought was a freind, sided with her, but I would,nt break down in front of her, nearing the home time I left the bench and went into the office, I was to hand my nottice in but they persuaded me to stay, and I took a couple of days off,on my return I gave up being a Bench head and went to another part of the factory, not having to share a tea break with her was heaven in it,s self, and it took six months before I got my confidence back, and was very quiet with everyone, and although i did come back to be me, it was never the same. I thank God that at that time I did,nt lower myself to her level, and that I did,nt cry in front of her. I cried many away from her, but I was hurt too of the people you think are your freinds, and they side with the one with the loudest shout, but I don,t regret it for one moment that I did,nt surcumb to the likes of her.

'I feel stronger now, and have learnt by this. I try to do my best to be freindly to all people whom I come across in life, I would say I,m a caring person, but something like this makes you wary of ever being totally relaxed with people, in the eye,s of some people I guess it would not be called bullying, I just know that I truely hope that I would never make anyone feel the way I felt. I was the age of fifty two at the time and she was younger than me, how did I let It happen? I can,t answer you that, why do we let ourselve be made unhappy by people like this? I know it was one of my unhappiest periods of my life. And I hope who reads this it will help because bullying in any form is unacceptable. These people are usually unhappy themselves, but still is no excuse to take it out on other people. I, ve been fortunate in my life that I do have some very close freinds that have stuck by me through thick and thin, they listen to me as it turn I listen to them, it,s freindship that has grown over many many years, they know me and I know them, what we says stays with us, and I do feel myself blessed. I hope this helps someone out there. Be happy and true to yourself.'

CASE TWO

(Written in 2007)

'I was quite new to my school and hadn't really made many friends. When on the last day of school a girl said that maybe we could sit together at lunch. I was quite happy because she was popular and could help me make friends. One day I was going to our condo pool when I saw her. We swapped phone numbers and talked about school. I invited her over to my apartment to get to know her. She didn't like many things I liked. After a few play dates I suggested that we could be friends. My sister and I caught the bus in the morning and afternoon. On the other hand she went by car. Since we were both friends we thought maybe we could both go on the bus together. After about a week she started coming on the bus. As you can probably guess we sat together and talked. She had three sisters, one also going on the bus. Her sister was younger than my sister but they still sat together.

'It had been about a month since we were first friends when we started to have fights. She found me annoying, bossy and mean. She wouldn't talk to me for days which made me unhappy and depressed. Then one day she started to kick and punch me. I told my mother and father and they said to tell the teacher if it kept on happening but to also try to sought it out myself. The next day she carried on kicking and punching me. So I said to her I would tell the teacher if she didn't stop. She answered "fine tell the teacher, I'm not scared of her." I decided to tell the teacher what had happened. I told my teacher what had happened but she did nothing to help the situation. I made peace with "Julie" and said to forget about what happened.

'After two weeks we had another fight. She ignored me and tried to annoy me. This time I wrote her a note saying I was sorry. After about two months, she and I had our third fight. This time she told children I was mean, bossy and not a good friend. My mother and father went to my school and told the year head what had happened. They didn't do much to help the situation. I learnt to ignore her and make more friends. It was the start of a new year and I saw two girls sitting together. I asked them if I could sit with them and they said yes. "Julie" told my new friends I was annoying, bossy and mean. One of my friends stopped sitting with us. This made me angry and sad. "Julie" started giving me horrible looks. That's when my parents went and spoke to the vice principle. My parents asked if I could be moved into a different class but they said it would be easier if I stayed in the same class. I have learnt lots of things from this experience and next time I will be more careful in choosing friends.'

CASE THREE

(Written in 2007)

'The bullying that most affected my family was to my third daughter—born many years after her sisters—so that she had an extensive vocabulary together with a very pronounced foreign accent—this was enough to cause annihilation with fellow students in a new primary school that she attended. Together with moving to a new state it was an incredibly difficult and upsetting time for her and culminated when two of the pupils said that they would be her friend if she would wait at the school gates for them—unfortunately, when she did they started hitting, biting quite fiercely and then tearing her dress. I can't tell you the dreadful feeling that I felt as a Mother and promptly telephoned the School Principal whose only comment was "well what do you want me to do about it?" I have to stress this was in the 80s so hopefully there is a little more understanding now—

'Actually there was a telling end (for us) to the saga in the fact that 25 years later my daughter, who was a professional, was in her Office when in walked one of the two protagonists—heavily tattooed and drugged out of her mind—I am especially proud that my daughter had let go of all the animosity and felt deeply sorry for the girl. (I can't be so forgiving)'.

CASE FOUR

'We are the parents of four sons & several years back I was appalled to discover our third son now in his 40's was regarded as a bully. I was told by a cousins daughter that she hated meeting him or his mates & since have heard of several others he bullied. Oh how I wish we had known & been able to put a stop to it. He has been in trouble with the police so being able to get away with it gave him power to do wrong. I wish we had that time over again. We were involved in all out sons activities, coached their sporting teams & were there for them.

'The other 3 have successful lives but we seldom see No 3 son now—he has 3 lovely children, never been married and recently his children were involved in a home invasion where they were terrorised. Talk about the sins of the father harming the children—bullying is hateful.

'I hope your book has a positive effect so as children like our grandchildren can hold their heads high and not feel shame for their fathers actions.'

CASE FIVE

'I am an old woman of 84 and I remember when I was 12, a boy round my age was always getting Bullied at school & on way home his father came up with a great idea, and taught him to fend of bullies by teaching him to box exit all Bullies. It is good idea to be able to beat these people at their own game.'

CASE SIX

(Written in 2008)

'I was a victim of bullying for 8 years at school at the hands of a spinster teacher, she taught me for 4 years. I am left handed and she beat me across my hand with a ruler & a small cane because I wouldn't use my right hand. I went to school eagerly but she made my life a misery there were other kids who were bullied by her too & I still know some of them, but she got her karma, she went totally blind before she died. She also sent me to get the cane for nothing & she had "pets" & they used to lie about different kids, not only me & we'd get the cane for nothing. She's get all the slow learners (no help those days) & call them horrible names & when a new headmaster came, she'd tell him all about the kids she bullied & we'd all get "picked on" then.

'We were taught to respect adults & teachers & I couldn't do folk dancing (one of my sisters is left handed & she had the same treatment by this teacher) & we'd always go up the wrong side & we'd get hit with the little cane & now I know I had low muscle tone (not diagnosable then) & the teacher's pets would throw the ball at my feet instead of to my arms & then say "Ann Scott dropped the ball" so out would come the little cane & she'd make me run even when I was a teenager at, the last day of school, I get 75 yards start in a yards race & still come last & she got some fiendish pleasure out of that. She bullied boys as well as girls, no-one questioned teachers' activities those days & Dad was on the Committee & involved with the school & the head teachers & working bees and there was only one good headmaster who took no notice of her & formed his own judgements, he was progressive for his time & he wasn't "cane happy". When I went back in 1989 for the 15th reunion I saw him & his wife & he was genuinely pleased to see me. I could never do anything right in her eyes & I believe that I have ADHD, as does "Michael" and "Phillip" so that didn't help so I was often sent outside & that's where my mental illness surfaced at school and wasn't helped by her tyranny. She taught mum at a different bush school but she didn't do it to Mum, Mum went to her funeral but I didn't & only a handful of ex-pupils went yet many of them still live in the "Warrington" area. I went over to "Beckham" from "Warrington" on the day of her funeral. I had trouble learning to write because of her, I was in Year 5 before I could write properly & the good headmaster got a lot of potential out of me & without the all the bookwork, I kept topping the class, there was only 12 kids in my class but there were 4 grades in each room so there were 40 plus kids in each room. Those days it was difficult with copybooks for left handers as there were no biros only scratchie pens with nibs & inkwells & blotting paper but left handers smudged their work. The greatest percentage of bullying she did was on left handers.

'When "Phillip" was at the ****** **** School he was bullied by other kids, one being my nephew (my 3rd brothers youngest son, is already 11), he had rulers (held down) stuck up his back passage, called "***** *****" by "Andrew" who at the time (about 8 years old) was still wetting the bed every night & "Phillip" hasn't wet his bed since he was 1. Both those boys ("Phillip" & "Tom") were toilet trained early because I did it & I see kids of 3 & 4 still in nappies nowadays. "Joan" spoke to my sister-in-law about it & I spoke to the teacher & she said, "He plays the victim.". My left-handed sister is only short & when she went to the "Warrington High" in 1981, she was bullied by a bunch of girls in Year 8.

'I know of one young fellow in "Warrington" Year 8 ("Mark's" age) who hung himself because he was a victim of bullying (13 years old) & no teacher would help him. When my youngest sister was at High School, in Year 12 she was bullied by an old spinster teacher, we lived in "Rosetown" then & despite Dad going to the Principal, nothing was done so she had to live with us & do Year 12 (1987) in a "Rosetown" high school.

'When I was at "Warrington High" there was a male teacher who was a paedophile especially with boys & many complaints were made but nothing was done & he even (after I left) he was made Deputy Principal he ended up in "Rosetown" still teaching & earlier this year I saw his funeral notice in the "Rosetown" paper. so you see why I'm so against the cane in schools. In my day it was misused.'

CASE SEVEN

(Written in 2008)

'I was heavily pregnant and still working full time as a nurse in a large state hospital. The woman in charge of the ward decided to target me. Every day she found fault with what I did when others would agree I had done nothing wrong.

'She would tell new staff that "I was a nice person but not to trust my work" My work standard was never in doubt in the numerous other places I had worked.

'On one occasion she told me to put something away as I had supposedly left a piece of equipment in the wrong place. A colleague immediately owned up to doing this, the bully then said "Oh my God—don't be like her" indicating me. It was not said in fun or as a joke but with malice and in front of the staff and visitors in the unit.

'I cried each day before going to work and would vomit each day when I got home.

'When I left to have my baby I told the area supervisor what had happened and how I had felt bullied and victimized and had been marginalized from the rest of the staff.

'I was told not to be silly, it was no more than a personality clash. Letters I had written to complain were shown to her but I was "Strongly advised" not to send them on.

'After the birth of my baby I went to work in a different department and have climbed up through the ranks where I am now in a senior position.

'Some time after I had left I bumped into a colleague from those miserable days. She apologized and confessed that she had believed all that had been said about me and admitted that she had no proof but the bully was convincing. She also confessed that the day I left and focus changed and she became the target, she too was bullied until she left.

'This particular bully has since retired but caused a lot of heartache during her career and ended quite a few careers prematurely".

While this is the end of this victim's story, she has added the following:

'Both my partner and I have been victims of workplace bullying.It is a destructive cancerous force that is eroding or work force. Having been bullied myself and also having been the partner of a bullied person I think that the effect of bullying on the family is something needing recognition.

'The family is usually helpless to do more than offer support which seems so inadequate.

'Life to a large degree revolves around the issues. Mental health all round takes a beating—not just that of the victim. but of those around.

'It has also come to my notice that once somebody stands up to a bully and reads the available literature, every one else who has an issue with bullying wants you on side for their case, again adding to the stress.'

The writer continues:

'I feel the only way to stop bullying (or mobbing . . . a better term) is to legislate against it. That way a bully is actually breaking the law.

'Bullying is reaching epidemic proportion, causing untold harm both mental and physical and costing millions of dollars to the workplace.'

CASE EIGHT

1 'There was . . . a boy at both Primary and High School, named "Andrew", now in the armed forces, who used to bully me—spit on me, bash me, destroy my property, graffiti on my School bag, mouth off, etc and I had fancied him in primary school. Years later . . . I bumped into him at a NYE event, he was fat and drunk—he told me that the reason he bullied me was because he liked me. He tried to pick me up that night and I did not go for it!

2 'There was . . . a girl at High School that was a bit of a dreamer, she used to draw clouds, my friends and I thought this was pretty funny so we would tease her about it. Years later . . . She was at a nightclub I frequented and she accosted me about the bullying and got pretty angry at me in front of my current friends. After she left the room, I explained what she said and what I'd done—my friends of that time laughed at it with me then, too.

3 'There was . . . a girl at Primary School, who used to annoy me no end but I never said anything until one day we were on a bus coming back from swimming and she was sitting in front of me, brushing her hair and flicking the water from her wet head on to me. I said "Stop it, Sleepy!" a few people overheard and the name stuck. One day during assembly her angry mum approaches me and says I have to go to the principal's office. So I did. The principal asked me to explain why I'd called her "Sleepy." I explained because it doesn't look like her eyes open much and she looks . . . sleepy. The principal actually laughed and dismissed the issue.

4 'There was . . . a group of girls that most would bully each other, but the ringleader was "Penny". One day she wanted to play a game, it involved standing in a circle and letting her hit us on the head. I was not up for this, but she manipulated all of us to keep us there and keep quiet to the

teachers. She would ask other people to play out her bullying for her and they did it! She would cheat off me in class and with homework, too. I don't know why the teachers would not stop her, the group had counselling with the School Counsellor and we were told to stop. It did not stop, "Penny" became more manipulative and secretive. Years later . . . "Penny" was still at it, even though we'd left school, she persists in trying to affect me until recently when I wrote her a nasty letter telling her to back off. Not sure of the effects of this letter, only time will tell. "Penny" is pure evil.

'Note: I attended Public Primary School from 81 to 85 & High School from 86 to 90.

5   'The first time I entered a chat room on the Internet I was bullied. What I experienced was like hate crime. Really nasty comments either about me directly or subversively. Every time I rejoin the "net scene" I am attacked because they think I am easy prey. Years later . . . I've learned not to care about insults that don't make sense.'

CASE NINE

(Written in 2008)

'I work as a carer at "redwood *****" in "abbeytown" for 18months. During this time, I have been subjected to bullying. The bullying started this year in April after I made a formal complaint about another carer for verbally and physically abusing a resident. In the time that this investigation was going on. I still continued to work. The staff were told to treat me as normal and not to speak to me about the incident.

'I was treated as a leper, the staff didn't want to talk to me, when I had to speak to the carers or RN,s or even "Jane",(the clinical manager) I was spoken to like a piece of crap.

'I could hear the staff talking about me, when the staff thought I was in a residents room, I could hear them with there snide remarks.

'To keep my sanity, I found myself hiding in residents rooms and break down.

'I knew in my heart I had done the right thing about reporting this carer, so why was I being treated like this.

'The investigation had finished, this carer was told she could no longer be a carer, she was able to still be employed only as a service staff.

'"Wendy Peters" (DON) drew a meeting and told the whole staff in front of me that "Mary Ross" will no longer be employed as a carer but as a service staff.

'I cannot explain to you how I felt, all eyes were upon me. I continued to work. The sniggering, the stares the stupid remarks people would make, the place was really doing my head in.

'I was going to my doctor every fortnight for councelling sessions. I told her everything that was going on at work. I couldn't help it but I broke down. I couldn't take it anymore. "Dr day" wrote me a sick certificate for

I week. I felt I needed that time off to try to find myself again, to breathe again, so to speak.

'In the time I had off, "Jane" (clinical manager) rang me to see how I was going and to ask me when will I be coming back to work.

'I told "Jane" that I will come back to work soon, I told her about the remarks staff were making and how I was spoken too. "Jane" said she would look into it and it wouldn't happen again.

'I also received a phone call from "Marg maxwell", she is another carer at "redwood *****".

'"Marg" is the only person other than my family and Dr who stood by me.

'I returned to work after having a week off.

'The atmosphere in the air you could cut with a knife.

'I was hoping things would go back to normal.

'The carer I was on with for the morning, "anne wilson"', we were changing a resident, the same resident that was abused by "mary ross". As we were changing this resident, "anne" said to me, I better be careful I might be reported.

'I just ignored her and continued.

'"Anne wilson" and "Sue cox" were the main carers that would start these stupid comments and really didn't care what it was doing to you.

'All the staff could see that "Marg maxwell" and I were good friends.

"So, to my horror, "anne", "Sue", "wendy", "jane" and certain RN,s were now attacking "Marg".

'She to was being spoken to like a piece of crap and ignored.

'"Anne" and "Sue" would see my car parked outside "marg's" house in "abbeytown", so when I took I week off work in may this year because there was a death in my family.

'When I came back to work, "anne" and "Sue" had told "Marg" that I had said horrible things about her.

'I was dumb founded as to why "Marg" had actually believed them. So more than ever now, I felt isolated.

'I was still continuing to see my Dr. "Dr day" had prescribed me anti depresants.

'My home life was in trouble, I shut my husband out and my children, I just wanted to shut myself away.

'I couldn't stop crying. I didn't want to go to work anymore. I loved my job but hated the people I worked with.

'I wanted to reach out and talk to someone.

'I felt hurt and betrayed that "Marg" had even considered that I would say anything about her, I thought she knew me better than that.

'I was going to my dr more often now.

'I returned to work, to find that "Sue" had written something in the communication book in the nursing home.

'She accused me of not showering residents properly. So in retaliation I wrote in the communication book. I had had enough.

'"Marg" and I started talking again and nothing more was said about the incident.

'"Wendy Peters" called a meeting for all staff, at this meeting, she said that NO STAFF ARE ALLOWED TO GO TO HER OR "JANE" OR THE RN,s ABOUT ANYTHING UNLESS IT IS TO DO WITH THE RESIDENTS.

'The bullying continued. I did go to many different RN,s about what was going on, they just informed me that we are all adults and need to grow up.

'So I went to "wendy" and "Jane".(I DIDN'T CARE WHAT SHE SAID AT THE MEETING).

'I was told by both of them they would talk to the staff involved.I told her of an incident were an RN raised her voice to me infront of all the residents because I was helping a resident get there breakfast.

'"Marg" and I continued to receive this treatment.

'If ever you walked past "wendy" shed totally ignore you.

'By this time it was august, I had atleast 5 shifts to work. By this time I had really had enough.

'I knew in my heart, I could not work there anymore.

'I went to my scheduled appointment with my Dr on august 13th, I told her I had had enough.

'I want to resign. So with my Dr,s help she wrote out my resignation.

'I took my resignation to "wendy" and "Jane", they both said to me, YOU ARE VERY, VERY SICK WHEN YOU FELL WELL AGAIN, YOU CAN COME BACK AS A CASUAL. Then I said to her that I didn't want to leave but I felt that I had no option, "wendy" replied by saying. JUDY, I CANT CHANGED MY STAFFS PERSONALITIES, I said I don't want you to, I just want you to stop them being bullys and making my life hell.

'THEY HAVE ALWAYS BEEN LIKE THAT, I CANT CHANGED THAT.'

'I told her I will never come back here and left.

'I am still seeing my Dr and I am still on medication.

'I am still good friends with "Marg" and I find my self helping her as she is still being bullied.

'I have found out that the staff are saying I resigned because I couldn't handle work and my children.

'This angers me because none of the staff will take responsibility for bullying.

'"Wendy peters" is the DON she is meant to protect her staff from being bullied.

'"Wendy" blantantly said to all of us that she doesn't want to know.

'I want to take this matter further, I felt I had no option but to leave my job.

'I want to be compensated for the money that I have lost out on and the fact that my family are struggling more now as a results for me not working.

'I want "wendy" and the rest of the "abbeytown" hospital to be accountable for the bullying and harrassment that caused me to leave my job'.

While this is the end of this particular story, this victim continues with the following:

'I am a mother of 6 children, my children have been in and out of several schools because of bullying and the most sad thing of all is that no one listens or cares.

'We have now moved to the country, they go to a smaller school.

'I at the moment am trying to contact TV stations and writing to the ombudsman with a case I am going through at the moment.

'I just recently resigned from my job as a carer in a nursing home due to being bullied and victomised.'

CASE TEN

(Written in 2009)

'My son "Matthew" was bullied at school in grade 5 to the point where he attempted to hang himself at school. But for the fact that the knot he tied gave way, he wouldn't be with us today

'For your information, a very brief outline: "Matthew" started grade 5, Bullies were in a gang, and bullied him mercilessly and unendingly. I spoke to his teacher several times in the 8 months up to his suicide attempt. Also spoke to the Assistant Principal. Both "promised" they'd deal with it. In August I wrote a letter to the Ed. Dept to complain that nothing was being done. As it happened, the day I was handing that letter in to the Principal was the day he attempted suicide. The school didn't tell me about it. I found out via a friend of "Matthew's" who had seen him hanging off the play equipment and had run to get a teacher. Six days after his suicide attempt, I miscarried a 16 week pregnancy. A year later we were still waiting for answers. We ended up at **** to access a report that we had requested from an investigation we had asked for which had been denied us.

'"Matthew" is in Year 9 now and happy at school. He has been taught coping mechanisms by a very good psychologist over a year and a half period. I was helped enormously and given reference to several very good books

'The mother of this victim, who submitted her son's story, said that her son wouldn't write a piece about being bullied because he would rather move on.

'This same mother has also been good enough to recommend a book about bullying which other victims and their families might also be interested in:

Bullying Solutions
By Helen McGrath and Toni Noble.

And here is the full story, also written and submitted by the mother of
the victim. A huge thanks for this.

'MY SON TRIED TO KILL HIMSELF. He was 11 years old at the
time. He wasn't depressed, nor previously suicidal, he hadn't made any
threats or given us any warnings. He was the victim of school bullying.
It had gone one, unchecked, for almost a year by the time "the incident"
happened. On the day he attempted to hang himself, he had simply had
enough. He tied a school bomber jacket around his neck and tied it off on
some play equipment that was a platform about 5ft off the ground. He
stepped off the platform and was seen by a friend to be hanging for about
15-20 seconds before the knot he tied came undone and he fell to the
ground. It sounds funny but I'll forever be grateful that I never enrolled
him in scouting! His friend raced towards him and she and another boy
chased my son around the school grounds until he ran into the boys toilets
and they went to get a teacher. This all happened at recess, which at the
school was between 10.30am and 11am.

'Want to know when I found out about "the incident"? When I picked
the children up from school that afternoon at 3.20—and a friend told me.
Not a teacher, the Principal or even a school counsellor. His friend! When
the bell went! She was distressed and crying and threw her arms around
me babbling something about "Matthew" (my son) trying to hang himself.
I didn't believe her, I thought maybe his hat strap had gotten caught on
something or he'd run into something anything but that he'd tried to hang
himself. It didn't in my wildest dreams occur to me that she was telling the
truth, that she wasn't exaggerating. Whatever was going through my mind
that afternoon certainly wasn't that my 11 year old son might have died
that day and the school hierarchy didn't think it important enough to tell
me about it. Nor in fact to even contact a member of the Department of
Education to find out what steps to take.

'What makes it even worse is that I was at the school at lunchtime
that day. I spent almost half an hour talking with office staff about
upcoming fundraising events (I, and my friend were the sole fundraisers
for the school of 250 students). I saw the principal, who by that stage
most certainly knew that one of his students had attempted suicide and
he said nothing. I spoke with the school secretary, who as the first aid

offer, most certainly knew that my son had tried to kill himself, and she said nothing.

'The bullying had been going on for 8 months, right from almost the first day of school. We had tried all the different strategies, bought books on how to handle it. We're pretty informed parents and we thought we were dealing with it properly, but the thing is, you can only do your part, you have to have the cooperation of the school too, and we didn't. It came to a head actually earlier the week of "the incident" when "Matthew" slapped his 2 year old sister. He loves his sisters and has never lifted a finger to hurt them. It shocked us to the core. He was so upset afterwards and that's when it call came tumbling out—the fact that this "gang" of 11 year old thugs was continuing their bullying. Depsite us talking to the school about it—to his teacher, to the Assistant Principal and to the Principal himself. Several times. As the school's fundraiser and being on the School Council, I was at the school a lot. I spent recesses and lunchtimes in the staffroom, taking cakes in for morning tea, enjoying the company of the teachers who often gave me their "wish lists" for fundraising. It was inconceivable that they would treat our concerns so lightly, but they did. "Matthew" knew that we had spoken to the school about it, he knew that they had promised to "deal with it", and that they hadn't. This gang of 11 year old bullies had gone so far as to threaten to hurt his little sister who was a prep student at the time. They had threatened to slash my car tyres and to come to our house and break our windows if he dobbed. How in god's name does an 11 year old come up with threats like that?

'But I digress. The day "Matthew" slapped his baby sister, my husband and I sat down and formalized a letter to the Principal, with a copy to the Education Department. I didn't like doing it because I believed I had a great relationship with the school. But I did it because my son came first. I held on to the letter for a couple more days until I could actually be at the school and physically hand the letter over. On the day of "the incident", after his friend had told me her story, (which, remember, I didn't believe), I asked "Matthew's" friend's dad to mind the 2 year old while I went and handed the letter about the bullying to the Principal. All the while, not knowing what had happened that day. At the office building, the Principal was coming out of his office when I arrived, and when he saw me he quickly ducked back into his office and shut the door! The Assistant Principal stood at his door, almost guarding it. She asked if she could help me. I handed her the letter and the conversation ensued thus:

'ME: This bullying has to stop, and I know you said you'd deal with it, but it's still happening. This letter is a formal complaint, and it's copied to the Education Department. I'm sorry, but "Matthew" is miserable.

'THE ASSISTANT PRINCIPAL: Right, good, right, well, this letter is good, we can do something about it now. "Matthew" told me today that you'd be giving me this letter. Um, did he tell you what happened today?

'ME: He has guitar lesson—I just saw him walking to it so I haven't spoken to him but his friend just told me some bizzare story about him trying to hang himself, what happened, did he get his hat strap caught on something?

'THE AP: Good, right, well this letter is good, now why don't you go home and talk to "Mike" (my husband, "Matthew's" dad) and we'll have a meeting about this in a week or so. Now, are we ready for the Trivia Night and the Father's Day Stall?

'Does that sound to you like they were attaching the "correct level of importance" to "the incident". To a child's suicide attempt? A child in their care? That's the only answer we got from the Department of Education after months of to-ing and fro-ing. That . . . *"The school, and the Principal hadn't attached the correct level of importance to the incident that occurred on that day with our son "Matthew!"* "The Incident". That really began to bug me. They kept calling it "the incident". It wasn't an incident. It was the day that my 11 year old son tried to end his life. The day he gave up trusting the teachers charged with his care would protect him. It was the day that my 11 year old son thought that dying would be preferable to being constantly harrassed and tormented by kids his own age. It was the day that, but for sheer dumb luck, my son would have died.

'When I got all my kids (at the time I had 5) home that afternoon, I took "Matthew" into the office and asked him what had happened that day. I said that his friend had told me a story about him trying to hang himself. He said: "I didn't try mum, I did hang myself but the jumper came undone and I fell and then everyone chased me and I couldn't find anywhere else that I could do it and then I had to sit in the office and play Jenga with one of the naughty kids then I went back to class and "Pete" laughed at me".

'"Pete" was the ringleader of the gang of thugs. "Matthew cried, I cried, I comforted him as best I could. I knew my husband would be on his way home so I didn't ring him, I felt something like this had to be said in person. I sent "Matthew" to have an afternoon snack and watch telly with the rest of his siblings. "Matthew" at the time was the middle child of five, two above him and two below him. They didn't know what had happened but bless them, they must have sensed something was up because their usual bickering was absent and the older two got snacks for the younger three and they sat quietly watching t.v., listening to music or doing homework. As for me, I don't remember the next hour. I remember looking at the clock on the wall in the office, I know that I threw up because there was vomit in the upstairs loo. The next thing I remember, an hour had passed and "Mike" was home.

'We talked together first, then with "Matthew", then with the older two kids. There were a lot of tears that night and a lot more hugs than usual. There was very little sleep on our part, mine and my husbands. We both kept getting up to check "Matthew", like we hadn't done since he was a baby.

'The Principal didn't *"attach enough importance to the incident"* to even meet with us that evening. When my husband tried to ring the school everyone had gone home. There was no answer at the education department and we didn't think to ring the police. The principal couldn't even be bothered meeting with us the following day. We started ringing the school at 8am and he was constantly "unavailable". He didn't call in any of the resources that the Ed. Dept boast they have. If a school burns down during the holidays, the very next day there are plans in place to make sure the kids' education isn't affected. If a teacher is assaulted by a student, immediately that teacher is counselled and on stress leave and the student is "dealt with". Our son tried to kill himself because the school was negligent in their care and the principal was too busy at a meeting "out of school grounds" with another teacher to even talk to us. We pushed the issue and the secretary tried to fob us off with a meeting a week in the future. My husband asked if she knew what had occurred the previous day and she admitted that she did but that the principal was "just too busy at the moment". We pushed harder suggesting that perhaps we should just ring the family lawyer first to see what we should do and surprisingly she arranged a meeting that afternoon.

"Matthew" had chosen to go to school. I couldn't believe it. My brave, beautiful son wasn't going to let those thugs deter him from his education or seeing his friends. "Mike" and I had a row that morning, quite unusual because we don't fight. I wanted to keep "Matthew" home and basically never let him out of my sight again. "Mike" wanted to let "Matthew" make the decision himself. In hindsight, "Mike" was right and I was just reacting. That morning, I walked up to "Matthew's" teacher. I am a *** in astrological star signs and I guess I must have been channelling all of that fury that day because she looked a bit scared of me. I said: *"You keep them away from my son today, I don't care if you have to manufacture jobs for him to do all day but you keep "Matthew" safe of I will come after you. You will see how angry I will be and you really won't like it".* Was I threatening her? Too damn right I was. She had been given 8 months to deal with the bullying. All the boys were in her grade and she even instituted a "bully book" for kids to write anonymously about being teased or bullied. She disbanded it because too many kids were writing in it naming this one particular gang! She even admitted it! Bizarre!!!

'The Principal and the AP finally met with us after recess. "Mike" and I went into that meeting full of the belief that they had been too busy to see us because they had been "dealing" with the consequences and putting things in place. We believed firmly that the Principal must surely have been in contact with the Ed. Dept and were arranging punishment for the gang and sorting out what to do next for "Matthew". HAH! The Dept of Education didn't even know about "Matthew's" suicide attempt until a school council member (a so-called friend of mine that I had called to tell her what had happened) rang them to find out if the school council could be held liable by us for what had happened! I have to say here, suing someone, suing anyone let alone the stupid school council hadn't even occurred to us and when it was offered to us later we refused. All we wanted was justice for our son and to hear that the school were sorry for not acting sooner. All we were concerned about was "Matthew's" mental health. My background comes from a B.A. with a major in Psychology and I had worked for Psychiatrists and Psychologists as a secretary while I was studying. I wanted "Matthew" to see someone but we believed that the school could access their enormous resources with the Dept of Education and something would be happening very soon. HAH!

'The Principal and the AP hedged around the issue, talking about how much our toddler had grown, whether my car was back on the road after a mechanical problem, whether "Mike" had enjoyed his recent trip to the United States for work. They talked about anything and everything except why we were there. We took control of the meeting. I got aggressive and slammed my hands on the conference table. I said that we wouldn't pussyfoot around, that we were very unhappy that it had come to this and that they had better deal with it. We told them that we wanted the ringleader of the gang, (the boy who had been the one to finally push "Matthew' over the edge) to be suspended. The Principal said that he couldn't do that, it was up to the Dept of Education to suspend a student (he lied!). We said that we wanted the two main bullies to be moved to a different classroom away from "Matthew", we reasoned that "Matthew" should be allowed to stay where he was because he hadn't done anything wrong. The Principal claimed that there was nowhere else for them to go (he lied!). We asked him to disband the gang of thugs in the playground, stop them from playing together, and hopefully that would stop them from bullying. The Principal claimed he couldn't do that. He said . . . *"That's not my job to do, but I will be meeting with the parents of all the boys concerned. "Matthew" has named them all this morning and I will tell them that they have to teach their boys not to bully. But you really mustn't mistake a bit of a biffo in the school yard as bullying".*

'Are you as shocked as I was at his lacksadasical attitude, his cowardly behaviour? Then, if you can believe it—he went on to warn us that we should be careful of the boys' parents. The school lies in an estate which is at a socio-economic disadvantage. That's what I've learned to say instead of that they're scumbag druggies and alcoholics, single parents with six different children to six different fathers, none of whom hold down a paying job and who should never be allowed to have children. It's the politically correct way to say that their sons can get away with being responsible for my son's near death. We, laughingly, live on the other side of the railway tracks. Get it—the wrong side of the tracks—them, and the right side of the tracks—us! Big joke eh?

'To further incense matters for me—over the next couple of weeks every time I turned around this ringleader—"Pete"—was at the principal's side doing the jobs that are given to the kids as rewards for achievement. It was almost like he was flaunting this kid in my face! I have to ask you whether you think I'm over-reacting here? Am I the only one who sees this man as blatantly incompetent? He is the Principal of a school. He has the power and the position to affect change and the changes needed to make the school a safe and happy place for the students there. Our son isn't the only one we know of who had been a victim of this gang. Other children have been bullied by them, some as young as preps. Several families had removed their children from the school as a result, and of course, it all came out afterwards didn't it—then the "incident" with our son became public knowledge.

'We actually have copies of letters written to the Principal and the school about the bullying. We also have copies of the Principal's response to them. In one case, he told the child victim's parents that their daughter had trouble making friends and that's why she felt she was being bullied.

In fact, these letters are why the Ombudsman took on our case. The Department of Education told the Ombudsman that there had been no other incidents of bullying at the school apart from the case of our son. The letters we have are all dated prior to what happened with "Matthew". The Education Department either tried to cover it up or were lied to by the Principal. Oops!

'You'd think that by now the Ed. Dept would have stepped in and sorted the school out. What a joke. Talk about jobs for the boys. The Officer assigned to our case was golfing buddies with the Principal. He even admitted that he didn't understand why he had been assigned to investigate the case as he and the Principal were friends.

'We had to push every step of the way for answers. They—the Ed. Dept—finally appointed an investigator. She turned up at our home after we were "TOLD" to make sure we were there on that day. Walked in late, and said: "I'm a psychologist, I'm an ex-teacher and I'm a mother, so I'm imminently qualified to discuss this little problem with you". Are your hackles up yet? Mine sure were. Then she proceeded to question us for 3 hours asking us to constantly slow down because she needed to write everything down. Our 2 year old was toddling around while she was at our home and she kept telling us: . . . "I don't want you to worry that you caused this, you're good parents". Bet you're shaking your head now! All you mums out there are probably ready to slap this woman. I know I was and I'm the most non-violent person you'd ever meet! Why on earth would she think we needed her to validate our parenting skills!

'When she finished interviewing us we asked when we would get a copy of her report. She made a show of opening her diary to show us how busy she was and talking about how long she needed to finish interviewing all the parties, collate her information and write her report. At no point did she tell us that we wouldn't be allowed to see the report. Then we asked about the protocol for suspending the boy who was the ringleader. She said "Oh I don't think that's necessary now do you? I'm sure he's filled with remorse. Besides, you dont' smack a dog a month after it wees on the carpet do you?"

'The report, as it turns out was denied us under the Freedom Of Information Act. We even fought it through **** and a lovely lawyer 'Roger Morgan of ****** ***** Solicitors who acted pro bono because he doesn't like "government bullies", and that's what he felt the Department of Education were doing to us. Unfortunately we were denied the report because it contained "personal information" regarding staff members. What a joke. What about all the personal information about our family???

'What annoyed us greatly was that at **** the Assistant Principal was being questioned by "Roger Morgan" and she kept saying "I really don't remember, it was several months ago". How many children in her care and protection have attempted suicide? How could she possibly forget? I will never forget. Nor will my family. It's etched indelibly in our memories. We'll never forget.

'I was pregnant at the time of our son's suicide attempt. I miscarried six days later. I was between 14-16 weeks pregant. It had been an otherwise healthy pregnancy. It wasn't pleasant, miscarriage never is of course, but even more so when it came about because of the stress of what had happened. I don't think "Mike" or I slept for about six weeks after "the incident", and so I guess I'm not really surprised. The hospital staff were wonderful. We told them what had happened and of course, while you could never stand up in court and say a miscarriage was caused by the stress of her son attempting suicide and the school's non-response to it, they all firmly believed that was the case.

'At the end of 2004 we gave "Matthew" the option of changing schools. He was in Grade 5 in 2004 and he chose to stay and finish grade 6 there. He wanted to graduate primary school with his friends. Once again, our brave son toughed it out. There were a couple of further incidents. One time I went to the school when a stupid boy pinned a note to my son that said "Kill Me I'm Suicidal Anyway". I took him home and kept him home for a week. When I complained to the school secretary that it had taken them an hour to ring me about it—she said "Why don't you just leave because you're such a troublemaker" Great attitude. It turns out later, and this is not gossip, it's fact, that she was having an affair with the Principal. How "days of our lives".

'I attended the Alannah and Madeline's Foundation's NCAB Conference in 2005. I just had to go. I felt that I needed to see that it was just that particular school that wasn't handling bullying. It was enlightening. It was around the time that **** upheld the Freedom of Information Decision to keep the report from us, so there was a bit of publicity, and it helped the conference anyway. I was amazed at the support from teachers and principals there though. I had complete strangers coming up to me to tell me that they were ashamed of their profession and felt that the principal should have been sacked! WOW! The funniest thing was that they felt the Department of Education were a "bunch of cowards" and that's a direct quote from a lovely female principal from another state that I sat next to in several workshops.

'I have to say that we lost a lot of faith in the teaching profession when this all happened, but it's slowly coming back. When our son went on to high school, we changed our daughter from that school to another. She seems to be okay there. There are a few bullying issues but we think we're a bit wiser now and jump on them straight away. I think they might even be scared of us, and do you know what. We don't care. They are responsible not only for the education of, but for the care and protection of OUR children. We have the right to demand that our children are safe.

'Now you're probably wondering about "Matthew". He's fine. Well as fine as a feral teenage boy can be. And you have no idea how much I love the fact that he's a teenage boy instead of a statistic. We arranged for a psychologist for him ourselves because the school and the Department offered nothing until months afterwards. They finally agreed to pay the costs. Whoopie Do! We still had to jump through hoops to get our money back though. It became such a pain to get the money back that we ended up paying most of it ourselves. I mean really, we had to justify to the Department of Education's insurers why we felt our son needed to see a psychologist. Hello??? He saw a team of two wonderful psychologists over a period of a year and a half then he made the decision himself that he was okay. He is still a bit sensitive towards bullying at school but he's getting a bit more resilient. He older siblings are very tough with him. They decided early on not to baby him and while I wanted to wrap him in cotton wool I had to take a step back and let them bicker and fight the way kids do.

'As for our family, well, we're a little sensitive about bullying at school and we aren't probably the best people to praise teachers to because we tend to not hold the profession in as high a regard as it probably should be held. We do try though and we try not to let our prejudice show when dealing with our children's teachers but they aren't all that bad.

'Our family has increased by 1. We are now 8—"Mike" and I and our six wonderful children. We had another baby in October 2006—"Todd". He doesn't replace the one we lost,—just ask any mother who has miscarried, but he is a character and he and big brother "Matthew" are real buddies.'

CASE ELEVEN

(Written in 2008)

'I worked at a local council as a casual admin assistant. I ended up being an all rounder & as my previous work had been in banking, I was utilised in the cashiering section quite often. There was a girl who had worked in the cashiers for approx 13 years. Not a very pleasant lady. As one of my kids said she looked like a sour puss, which ended up being more than true.

'I don't think she liked it that I could do the job without any trouble & that I balanced all the time. When she was out at the end of the day, she would make me find it as she reckons I needed training in this area, to know what to do & where to find it. She use to say that she was the boss as she had been there for so long & that I was just a casual.

'She would constantly have 2 sets of rules. One for her & one for me, & they were based on her mood for the day. She could never talk civilly to me, didn't like that I was better at cashiering than her & that I would get praise from the boss as I could work in any section.

'She ended up being down right rude to me every day & would say things about me to other staff. Everyone seemed to be scared of her & no one had the balls to stand up to her, even the boss. She seemed to have something on everyone so it seemed & she used it to her advantage.

'If ever I was on the phone, she would have a go at me, as she was the only one that could sit around & do nothing. She would take off without telling me & go to the shops or go home & expected me to cover the work load & to cover for her. She made life unbearable. I was sick to the stomach every day & suffered from migraines etc because of worrying about what she would do to me on the day.

'It seemed no one else would stick up for me as they were all scared of her & she was queen bee around the place. I ended up leaving there, which was a few years ago, but have since found that her marriage split up (which didnt surprise me as she treated her husband like a dog), & she no longer works at Council. If only I had had the guts to stand up for myself, I could have still been working there & nearly had long service leave.

'I also worked for a boss who would bully, harass his staff & his partner in the business. He would say sly things all the time. These had sexual undertones & he was always nasty. It depended on his mood for the day as to what kind of day the rest of us would have. He had us all on tenterhooks that his partner in the real estate would always be sick. He never had the balls to stand up to him. I was employed as a casual but worked a set 4 days a week. He had already chased off 8 girls who had previously worked at various stages for the company.

'The partner knew who had the problem but like I said he didn't have th balls to stand up to him. In the end I left & the other girl who worked there left after 23 years of service. They haven't been able to hold onto staff since as this bloke with his horrible wife kept chasing off good staff'.

CASE TWELVE

(Written in 2005)

'Our Grandson loved his school at "Harrison".

'I gave my daughter a block of land at "Walliston" near school worth $50,000 she built on it & they moved My grandson went to school nearby so my grandson quiet was bulled by a "Richard Bailey" and Mates.

'I took him back to my place 44 Acs at "Harrison". & sent him to school he lived with me & my husband & I took him to Local police club & was also taught how to defend him self. 3 yrs. I thought they'd kill him 1st lesson so my husband took me to milk shake & club he came home and was happy and says I'll show you put me on my back.

'Can Kill a person if not careful. So went home weekends and met "Richard Bailey" who picked on "Todd's" little sister "Jane"'.

"Todd" threw him over the fence they all kept away.

'"Jane" has learnt since a married young woman.

'My daughter eventually came back home to my place on the Farm lived in Relocatable 1st with me Huge Farm House later all went to another state.

'He had his Son Taught age 14 yrs Where I followed years later after my husband died cancer'.

CASE THIRTEEN

(Written in 2006)

While the following was written by a victim, it is more a comment and opinion than a case history.

From the victim: 'So glad to see someone taking an interest in this cancerous phenomena so prevalent in Australia. As an Aussie I am filled with an enormous amount of feelings (all negative)regarding this destructive situation here. No more so than in my state. I have responded to the bullying taskforce here, and a number of other govt initiatives to 'look into' this necrotic affair and you know what? All of the enquiries go absolutely no where. I have had a number of my submissions and recommendations even printed but nothing changes. I am of the firm belief that the Government cant afford to address it correctly for fear of civil action which would render the government (state and federal) bankrupt. I have endured and survived (if you could call it that) years and years of untold pain and suffering because I would not sit down and take what was dished out to me in the form of bullying. It comes right down from the top and management pick up on the benefits to themselves because not only can they feed their egos but they are comforted by the fact that they will get away with it because it is the status quo and because their is no 'superior' who will challenge that behaviour. Nursing is the worst, talk about eating its young, nursing is purely cannabilistic and infantacidal with what it does to its neophytes (teaches them to encorporate bullying practices as a form of management practice). I could go on forever with my experiences to the extent that I even had my life endangered (along with my young daughter) and I am not the only who has had to endure this. And the worst thing is, there is no comeback for us victims. It is such an encompassing situation because it covers, health (wholistic), relationships, legal, employment and socialisation. I am very interested in what it is you are doing and what you hope to achieve from it. Unfortunately I know of one particular person who was doing her thesis on this and inadvertently uncovered some major deliberate design faults in government policy (to protect them from their own bullying practices) and before she could finish her doctorate, she was told it would not be considered as an appropriate project. Could this have been because the Uni was government funded? One can only speculate A! HOpe you achieve some positive and practical changes within the Aus government management and practice psyche'.

The following was written by the same victim, in 2009.

'I know it's been a few years since I was so traumatized by the bullying in the north, I have moved and the bullying, and whilst it still exists, I seem to think it is not near as bad here than further north. Maybe I am getting battle scared and don't get so effected anymore—either iether, my life is less traumatized by bullying.

This victim continues, also in 2009:

'Actually the most recent bullying episode for me was @ 12 months or more ago when a 'international' nurse who was promptly made Team Leader denegraded my Autralian customs because I was refusing to dob in a workmate. I went to her to address a matter of appalling nursing practice which I had witnessed. I didnt want him named because he was not the only nurse conducting practice to such poor standards. In my opinion it was a unit defecit in the standard of nursing practice within that unit. I felt it terribly unfair to name him when he wasnt the only one (it was a systemic issue) and I felt he didnt need to be targeted. I tried to explain to her how difficult it was for me as an Australian to dob in a mate (especially when I didnt believe he should be the only one targeted). To cut a long story short, she told me that Australia now is a multi cultural society and there was no place anymore for my AUstralian customs. That was a great comment coming from a foreigner. I was so insulted and upset, I went to the union and his response was amazing. He totally understood my dilemma and correctly reported my line of command and their ethnic background. None of which were Australian. I had no one to take this issue to because there was NOT one Australian nurse in the management chain so my issue soon died in the water. Her bullying continues and nothing has changed.

CASE FOURTEEN

(Written in 2007)

'I suffered from bullying from the age of 6 till I was 29 years old—I'm 54 now.

'I was born with one leg shorter—had to wear a built up boot 1 1/2" taller than the other one. I was very short 4' 8 ¼" tall and I had protruding teeth, from those years at school then at work my life was a total hell—

'I was constantly called names like "Hello ***** **** Where is your sister *** ******" to—"*******"'—I was constantly everyday tormented at school—then when I went to work because there was so much bullying through out my school life I didn't finish year 10, so the only work I could get was factory work—the bullying didnt stop. I was intimidated that much that I had a nervous breakdown in 1981 and I've been on the pension every since.

'Those people took away my dream—I had longed to have been a doctor, but by the time school finished my confidence was zero and I couldn't sit for the exams, and all the work I could get was in a factory, and the hell continued there as well—

'Growing up people laughed and tolerated and made excues for bullies. its no laughing matter—and there should be zero tolerance and no excues; for bullies—

'I'm still affected today—many years after it happened—Its scarred my life and I lost a dream that I had cherished.

'People only look on the outside, they dont see "me" "Mary"—inside, some who can love and care deepley, have a sense of humour—is a deep thinker and would love to help people. I have felt so lost—so alone most of my life—they can take away my dream, my life—my loves, but they won't take away my spirit—I have a right to be here—I have a right to be'.

CASE FIFTEEN

(Written in 2009)

'I came to live at a small Complex of 24 villas, which was built by the people from the Church. All the Villas have since been sold to private owners, & although it was called "Wirra Retirement Village"—the present Committee say it is not so, & consequently we get no help.

'I realised this when I bought in as my daughter was a Community Health Nurse & had patients here.

'The reason she recommended it was that she & her brother lived nearby & would care for me. I was 85 at the time.

'We have been involved in Caring for the Aged for many years, with my late husband being an Ambulance Officer, & five of my family are Registered Nurses, or have been. Three of my grandchildren still Nursing.

'I took on many jobs (voluntarily) to care for Aged people at Caring centres (26 years) also supporting the "Jarrabong" Society for disabled for many years.

'When I came here there was no number on the letter boxes—(they had fallen off), so I rang the Secretary of Owners Committee & asked what could be done about it. He gave me the phone no to ring the Strata Manager, who arranged to have the number replaced. I mentioned it to the Committee & nothing was said. I also asked for the name "Wirra" to be put on the entrance—offering to pay for it if necessary. The Strata Manager said it wasnt necessary or me to do that, but we kept getting the Financial Reports & the sign writer never seemed to get paid, so I sent a cheque. Since then they have treated me very badly. Firstly I became a member of the Committee & was appointed Secretary. I tried to run things properly as I had always done, & there was Petty Cash fund, only $100 I know, but I used to ask for a Report at the meetings. I never got one! Also there were only 4 members on the Committee at that time. I know there should have been 5. One day the three other members arrived at a meeting, at my place, with a letter already typed, asking a young couple to vacate one of the units as they were not 55 or over. I refused to sign it, because there was no discussion with me. These people were foreigners & had not been here long. The young man was never told he had to be over 55 & as I said there was no sign to say this. I still don't know how old he is, but his wife is a Dr of medicine & they were very nice people.

'When it came to the AGM. in 2006, I was again appointed to the Committee & the former Treasurer was absent, but sent a letter saying she would be Sec & Treas. so once again we only had four people on the Committee.

'When this lady came back & we had our usual meeting, all three resigned saying they couldn't work with me. I stood firm & said I wasnt resigning, as the only thing they had against me was that I asked for a Treasurer's Report—so I was left the only one on the Committee! The Strata Manager said we had to resolve the problem, so all three quietly came back on the Committee. There is no meeting room here, so we have very little socialisation. I have tried by having a get together at Xmas etc but that is all. We used to meet for morning tea at the other side of the property, & one day the Sec/Treas told me we were not allowed to talk "business" at the get together. A gag! Anyway finally this lady asked me if I would give 100% support to her. I said I couldn't. Ive never known a meeting where one could not dissent. If a proper vote were taken & we knew where we stood! Since then I am ignored insulted. My health broke down & I had a Pace-Maker put in & can't go to the meeting. I have nominated my daughter as Proxy & she attends when she can.

'There are two entrances to this property, 7 villas on this side & 17 on the other. The property is horseshoe shaped with several town houses in between. We as owners are not consulted about what is being done. A pine tree had to be cut down as neighbours complained, but they also cut down a lemon tree, which was the only one we had.

'Also the Committee had Real Estate signs taken down & one villa near me has been on the market for 2 yrs'.

The following was also written by this same victim, in 2009:

'I have reached my 90th birthday & am in pretty good health.

'Things have not improved much for the residents of this Complex.

'We have a new Sec/Chairperson but the former Sec is still on the Committee, but has all the say! The chap who has been in the Chair for only a few months was at the last meeting I went to. The lady, ex Sec, took the meeting & all he did was read the minutes of previous meeting!

'He has done some work in the gardens, has the muscle for it, but doesn't know a lot about plants. We had a lemon tree just on the unseen boundary of our two properties & it was chopped down—without any consultation with us—then a young lime was taken out & I'm sure he/ didn't know what it was—so everything appears to have a short back and sides in our grounds. Reminds me of a prison!'

CASE SIXTEEN

'A STORY ABOUT BULLYING

'Where I work in "Wimborough", there are 2 bully type women, over 50 years of age. "Jenny" was very nice to me for about 6 mnts, then she tried to intimdate me, by saying "The boss will yell at you, he will tell you off". My first thought was, "'Jenny' you must be mentally ill". I also thought she must be crazy in the brain, as I'm not frightened of the boss at all. "Jenny" then tried to critize my work and find fault, so I found fault with her work . . . "Jenny" was so shocked, she slunk back to her machine. When "Jenny" tried to tell the boss's daughter to tell on me, I shouted at her in front of the boss's daughter to tell "Jenny" certain information to do with work. "Jenny" backed down to me and slunk back to her work station. Bullies are usually cowards.

'In the newspaper in Wednesday's paper is a section about medicine. The doctor stated in July, 2005 that bullies are mentally ill. Their odd behaviour is:

1 Intidition
2 Critical (of work, appearance etc)
3 Telling lies to (Boss, Headmaster, etc)
4 Temper tranturms

'"Jenny" does fit this pattern. "Jenny" is unfortunately a very jealous, envious, spiteful, hates most people if she doesn't get her own way. The woman who had the same job I do before me, gave into "Jenny", and now "Jenny" completely dominates this other woman by telephone. The other woman is retired from work but is too frightened to stand up to "Jenny". Other people in this factory think they are great friends, but they cannot see the true relation ship. "Jenny" is afraid of me, as I stood up to her. "Jenny" is a true bully coward.

SECOND STORY ABOUT BULLYING

'The other so called friend of mine I made about 10 years ago in a factory in "Debton". This woman "Rose" come across as a nice, calm person. I believed that "Rose"' was telling me the truth about her sister, friend, etc. I met her sister twice about 5 years ago. I started work at this "Wimborough" factory where "Rose" had worked. "Rose" had told me she was reting from work in. "Rose's" sister "Meg" worked there too, "Rose" never mentioned her sister "Meg" had worked there too. As "Rose" had retired from work, I became friends with "Meg". "Meg" said her sister "Rose" was the sister from Hell. "Meg" being an easily frightened person was an easy target for "Rose" to dominate.
"Rose's" bullying takes the form of:

1   Telling lies about people
2   Playing one person against the other
3   Temper tanturms
4   Jealousy
5   Critical of her sister's friends, men etc

'"Rose" came back to work in the "Wimborough" factory. "Rose" being a very insecure person, started telling lies about me around the factory. Like telling the supervisor that her sister "Meg" didn't want to have lunch with me. "Rose"' was very jealous because according to "Meg", she wasn't allowed to have a female friend. "Rose" would tell the boss's wife and daughter, some terrible lies about "Meg" so they would not speak to her for weeks. "Meg" being physically gifted could pick up the vibrations from the boss's wife and daughter, just by their dark disapproving stare. "Rose" told balant lies to me about "Meg", "Rose" told me not to say anything to "Meg". I did ask "Meg" about these so called incidents, they were just made up lies. "Rose" is unfortunately an extremely jealous, full of lies, sly, individual personality. People who are secretive come across as a dishonest person. "Rose" is very secretive and I have gradually found out about her untruths to me. I still work with her, watch her different moods and assess my answers. I do not trust her any more, I only tell her what I want her to know like she does to me. Her sister "Meg" has retired from work and has exiled "Rose" out of her life. "Rose" has not caught on that "Meg" never intends to contact her ever again. "Rose" has laughed behind "Meg's" hair on all the cruel deeds she has done to her, thinking "Meg" doesn't know. Well, I might have to tell "Meg" later on, that her games of lies, playing "Meg" against other people so they wouldn't speak to her, throwing a temper trantrum at a wedding because "Meg" had a female friend, "Meg" will have the last laugh. "Rose" at work, has also told lies about me to the boss, (queer looks he gives me) tried to critize my work, I critized hers, she didn't like that. "Rose" does all this, because I made friends with her sister. "Rose" will be out of my life soon as I will get work in a different occupation. Bullies are selfish personalities and eventually end up all alone'.

CASE SEVENTEEN

(Written in 2007)

'When I was in High school—yr 9—I was bullied. I was 14 yrs old. I had the usual name calling but then it got worse. I got "Love Letters" that got my hopes up but were dashed when the return address turned out to be vacant Land. Then I started to get crude, rude phone calls which did'nt last when my dad answered the phone. I guess the biggy for me was when a hot pie was thrown at my face followed by bits of creambun. I think my parents when to the school and the physical stuff stopped but not the name calling. Needless to say, I stayed at school 'til my 15th birthday—August of that year. then I walked out at lunch time. My parents told me I could leave if I got a job. I did the next day.'

CASE EIGHTEEN

(Written in 2007)

'I was bullied at school—and I'm sure I fully deserved it. I was an only child, not used to mixing with other children, a loner. I wore a horrible brown cardigan knitted by an old lady who only had brown wool and brown was my least favourite colour. My favourite was pink. I had straight dark brown greasy hair and spectacles and a very plain face with a nose long and bumpy—a school mate's mother aid that was the only bit of character in my whole face. My skin was greasy too and I had no dress sense, my clothes were always awry.

'My surname, "****", didn't help. The boys would shout, "Here' cones ****" or "*** ***." They would hold me up as I walked from school to the bus stop and push me in the hedge or the nettles, make me pull my knickers down and laugh at them, or tell me to reach for the sky "higher, higher!". I learned to run so fast to get away from them that I became the best runner in the school and when I started winning prizes on Sports Day for the 100 yards, 250 yards, long jump, etc. I got cheered by the same boys who had bullied me, along with the rest of the school. They cheered me on year after year, by which time, a boy had joined the class whose surname was "*******", which totally removed any remaining heat from me—and onto him.

'I would advise any child who is being bullied to find a way to earn the respect rather than the contempt of the bullies. Find a way to excel at something, not necessarily come top of the class, but top in at least one subject. Boys are often urged to fight back and if they lick the bullies that gains great respect, but it's different for a girl, she has to find another way. I learnt this by accident; no one told me—I wish they had—it would have saved me a lot of tears and fears in those early years and made life a lot easier for me.'

CASE NINETEEN

(Written in 2007)

'When i was 13 i attended "Woburn" High School, i had many friends at that time and i used to go away with my family on vacations during the school holidays everything was great then one day 8 days after mt 14th birthday my father suddenly died at work he just collapsed no one knows why, one minute he was happily singing his heart out the next he was lying on the floor his heart had stopped and no body at that time knew first aid, so he was without oxygen for 11 minutes and he then went into a coma for nearly a fortnight and then my mum was asked to turn off the machines as he would have no quality of lif. I returned to school a couple of weeks later on finding that my friends were no longer speaking to me, as the days rolled on the kids at the school started to turn against me for a reason i don't know why, i started to wag school to try and find my own place where i could be alone and grieve for my dad, on the days i did go to school again i would be teased by the older kids because my father had died and told ugly things like now my dad was dead i could go with any guy i wanted to. i don't understand why they all turned on me, i do know that one of the year 11 students was the eldest sister of one of the girls who was my friend and she had taken a couple of days off with me, for the reason she was hoping to cheer me up as i become a recluse without my dad. I decided to go to school on this day that i proberly should of stayed home because when i got there i hadn't even gone through first period when i was cornered and confronted by the older sister of my once friend and told to leave school now or get beaten up by the entire years 10-11-and 12. They wanted to hurt me so i ran and i ran until i got home then i hid under my bed until my mum got home from work then i explained to her what had happened and so she raced down to the school with me in tow and yelled and screamed in disgust at the principal that she was appalled that things like this could happen especially as i had just lost my dad and she a husband we did not need any more stress in our lives at this moment So mum took me out of that school and enrolled me in "Oswald" High School, where i had to travel by bus for several months from 'woburn" to "Oswald" until we moved house. this is true to fact and i hope this never happens to any one else because i could not imagine that people could be so nasty and vindictive but i was totally WRONG'.

CASE TWENTY

(Written in 2007)

'My son was bullied in Primary/High School and also in the workforce by the Son-in-Law of the boss. It all came to a head in July last year when he had a breakdown he hasn't worked for the last twelve months which has been a big strain on him and his family. He has been having treatment and our hope is that he will be able to go back to the workforce and face the world again'.

CASE TWENTY ONE

(Written in 2009)

'To give you a background and paint the picture of my family I am a happily married woman (25 years) with two children. My second child became a victim of bullying when he went into grade 3. This particular year he was put into a composite grade with grade 4's. He is a child that has been often described as social, outgoing and intelligent. My son is taller than the average child by far. Our experience was initially quite devastating but as time has progressed the implications of this experience had a far deeper impact than I could ever have imagined.

'The primary school my children attended was a small school of approximately 250 children in a treed, semi-rural quiet community. Initially, everything went smoothly, there were rumblings of bullying but none that greatly affected my children. My daughter did come across as "bitchy" and "cliquey" young ladies but nothing her character couldn't handle. My daughter would just walk away and was happy to spend time in her own company. We have brought our children up to never give in and to always see any commitment through to the end whether it be a season of basketball or a term of music. To instill this into our children was important to us.

'I was actively involved in the school attending classes to help with maths, spelling, reading etc. I attended school excursions, my husband attended camps. Fund-raising was something I slowly moved into, raising $8,000 at one event I shared with one other mother and hundreds of dollars over the years.

'Over the years I felt I had a rapport with the administrative staff, teachers and principal. A number of incidents occurred with a grade 2 teacher while in my presence, which were damaging to the school and duty of care issues were brought about. I was asked to put in a formal complaint by the principal, which of course I did. I was also given the guidelines of the Department of Education which was that any complaint would be held in the strictest of confidence. I kept my word and to this day that teacher's reputation remains intact. This teacher was brought before the Department of Education and worked with for the following 8 months which was the remainder of the school year. I had confidence that the school would handle this teacher and guide this person to be a more responsible carer in the future.

'At the end of grade 2 my son came home with who is teacher was, and, who was in his grade from his friendship list for the following year. The school's policy was that the child was to write down the names of 4 of their friends so that the next year they would be comfortable joining the new grade with at least 1 or 2 of their close friends. My son was given the last child on his list (which was a girl), he said he put her down because there was a space left and he liked her. The class my son was put into had an older male teacher who had been at this one school for far too many years, he was renowned for his skills in maths and science (but with social aspects he was extremely lacking). My daughter had this teacher and we felt he would not suit our son at all.

'We were upset with the choice the school had made and felt if we approached them they would understand and make the necessary changes for the benefit of our child. We understood that if all the parents weren't happy and they granted everyone's wishes then how could they be expected to function efficiently. They guaranteed us that if my son was not happy and settling in well in the first few weeks they would gladly change him.

'The bullying started almost from the first day my son started in this grade, I feel that because my son was such an outgoing presence a couple of the grade 4 boys tried to pull him down a few pegs. It started with nasty comments like "what's that smell" when my son walked by their table, even to the point of asking my son's peers if they could smell it too! My son's peers would initially not make a response but in fear of being bullied themselves they would agree. In the playground my son was fine amongst his friends, but once back in class the subtle bullying would begin again.

'My husband and I were not happy with how our son had withdrawn and he confided to us what was happening. I approached the school and informed them that our child was not suited to this grade and asked that he be changed as they had promised. We told them what had been happening and they asked to let them deal with it and they would talk to the parents of the children involved. True to their word they did but the bullying didn't stop, it got worse! It then progressed to pushing back their chairs when my son was walking between tables to kicking him in the back of the legs when he walked past. In the playground they sought him out, pushed and shoved him and tripped him over, and when my son told them to "back off" they said "what are you going to do, tell your mummy!?" I didn't realise the extent of what these boys and the school had done to my child until I went in to tuck him in one night and he said to me "Mum I just want to die and go to heaven, it is happy there". He had not told me the extent of what had been happening to him. To hear these words from my little 8 year old devastated me my world came crumbling down. You nurture your children, teach them, bring them up to believe the world is good and through 8 year old eyes his little life was a mean, horrible place to be.

'I approached the school the next day with a passion and drive to have justice prevail. I was told they had addressed the issue and perhaps my son contributed to the bullying. Not happy with their response I approached the Department of Education to handle what I felt the school couldn't. From that day on my son was victimised and I was phoned every second day to say that he was in the principal's office for any minor thing!!!!

'In between times we needed to get an idea of whether the school was seeing something in our child we weren't seeing, so we sought out a child psychologist. We had several sessions over the next few weeks with her, both with me present and my son on his own. Our psychologist told me that she found my son to be extremely intelligent, outgoing, confident and deeply traumatised by the events of what he had experienced at the school. She suggested that she should talk to the school. The next day I received a call from her to say that she had approached the school and in her professional opinion (although she had never advised it before as she had always been able to resolve matters) she said to me "Get him out of there" never before in her professional career had she come across such a school with such disregard for a child.

'I collected my son at lunch time that day and he never went back! That was the best decision my husband and I ever made! I took my son to a larger school close by with a male principal. He gave us a tour of the school, he was so kind and gentle to my boy I had to choke back the tears. While my son walked ahead I gave the principal a broad outline of what my son had been through and he turned to me and said that no child should suffer or feel unsafe and it was the school's responsibility to guarantee that. I think I fell in love with that man with every word he said. He took my son to all the grade 3 class rooms and asked him if he had a choice which class would he be in! Hallelujah! My son was ecstatic! It was so hard go get him to look at another school but this wonderful, caring man made him feel so welcome. He explained their school aims and curriculum and finished with their zero tolerance to bullying. Believe me after moving my son there definitely was a ZERO tolerance to bullying! Through my son's years at this new school I know of 3 children who were suspended for at least 3 days for bullying and then made to write a letter and give it to their victim. There was no back and forth banter with the parents. It was a Thursday when I took my son this school and I was going to enroll him to start on the following Monday. The principal turned to my son and said to him we have a fantastic children's author/illustrator coming to the school tomorrow (being the Friday) I would love if you could come in tomorrow! My son turned to me and said "Please Mum!" silent tears rolled down my face. "Of course" I said. We never looked back. My son was put into the class of his choice with a wonderful teacher who made my son "Star of the Week" for his first week. Each day he had to bring in either his favourite things, family photos, funny stories etc at the end of the week he was given a book with a page written by each child in the grade saying what they thought of my son. I have never been so happy reading this book. The transformation in my child was immense. I used to pick him up each day dreading what he would tell me of the days events, but all of a sudden the knot in my stomach disappeared, instead of tears of frustration and empathy I had tears of joy!!!!!!!!!! In grade 6 he was voted school house vice captain.

'What frustrated me the most was that the new school's simple, strong policy, without fear of backlash, was the best thing for my child. The best advice that I can give to any parent is that the devil you know isn't always better than the devil you don't. Never except what is happening to your child, seek professional help if it is advised, but you know your child and the decisions you make for your child can affect their future. My son is now in secondary school and although very happy, holds himself back from anything that could make him appear "different' or stand out in the crowd. He is a straight A student, he is often put forward by teachers to do advanced learning but he refuses because he is in a comfortable place socially and does not want to be seen to be different in anyway. He says to me "Mum, just leave it, I'm happy". My husband and I are just happy to see our son content with his life and where he is in this world. We know that the scars of the past are still there both for my son and myself.

Thankfully there was a school out there not afraid to deal with bullies as they should be dealt with. My son's Secondary School has the same policy and it works extremely well!

'One thing that was strange was that once I left this the first school, parents still at the school would pretend they didn't see me when shopping. Still to this day I am seen by some mothers as a defector even though I have never put the school down in anyway. People asked me why I changed my child's school and I just told them the new school better suited his style of learning. What was also amazing was that after I pulled my son from school, parents with past students at that same school came out of the woodwork to tell me of their bad experiences, but I had never heard them before! If only I had known. I know a friend who's 16 year old son was on antidepressants and seeing a psychologist who found that the majority of his problems stemmed from being bullied during his primary school years at that school. I feel guilty for being misguided and, on the flip side, proud that we made the change when we did.

'I do not feel any animosity towards the children who bullied my son, only against the system that failed to protect him. In a way the system was not protecting the bullies either—just teaching them you can get away with some things in life'.

CASE TWENTY TWO

(Written in 2008)

The following is an opinion followed by an experience, both written by the victim.

'To Whoever Reads This.

'You know what I'm sick of, I'm sick of all the bullying that has happened throughout my life and others so this is why I'm writing this.

'I am only writing this because I am disgusted by all the bullying that has happened throughout my whole schooling. This letter is for all those who have been bullied throughout their whole life and cannot get any space from the constant bullying.

'I myself come from a whole day of either seeing someone get bullied or get bullied myself, but then when I get home I still have to put up with bullying, so when I get home I don't get to rest or relax, for everything I do is being watched like a hawk, if I do anything wrong I get into trouble because somehow I have done something wrong.

'My wish is that one day the world will be in peace from the constant bullying from others.

'I think bullies are just cowards looking for a thrill by bullying people smaller and weaker than them, that's why those smaller and weaker people have trouble getting to sleep at night, because of all the horrors that have happened to them, and we the smaller and weaker people have to try and deal with it all, but sometimes we can't, and every time we have gone to fight back we are the ones that get in trouble, not the bully, but us the victims who get in trouble for fighting back, that's why some of us bullied people run away, or go and end their life.

'I am sick of it all, I am sick of hearing all the deaths, all the suicides, all the heart breaks, all due to bullying from some low life scum that thinks he's cool because he is able to pick on someone smaller and weaker than themselves, but all they are doing is ruining someone elses life and pushing them over the edge, making them think that suicide is the only way out, and if they do commit suicide then those bully's actually decide to think of what they have done to that person and how they pushed them over the edge, but then there are other cases where the victim lashes out at the bully's and then the victim gets into trouble for lashing out, it is like as though everyone else protects the bully's and just wait for the victim to lash out then get them into trouble, but, you do, the victim the one who tries to put a stop to it all, but in the end it feels like you can't do anything to stop what has already begun.

'I myself have been bullied by teachers and other students, here is a scenario: the other students in the class have started to pick on me, then the teacher decides to laugh and not tell the other students to stop, sometimes the teacher does tell the students to stop but they only stop for around 5 minutes then they start again making you more and more depressed or angry, which can either make you lash out or run out of the classroom and run off to a place that feels safe but in the end we still have to go back to the world of bullying where you can't escape, even when you do the right thing, you can't stop it all you can do is try, to try and stop it all but it feels like in the end you can't stop it.

'The bullying will just keep going on and on and on, but one day I hope that it might stop, this would make the world a whole lot better, but for now we have to try and get away from the bully's that coward together and can't pick on anyone their size and have nothing better to do than pick on people that are weaker than they are.'

CASE TWENTY THREE

(Written on various dates in 2005 and 2006)

11th December 2005

'I would love to share my story with you about being bullied at School it has caused me sevear emotional problems as an Adult and I still to this day almost 10 years after finishing school find it hard to make friends some of the things that happened to me were.

- I was Dacked(pants pulled down) in front of people on School oval underwear and all and a teacher just stood by and did nothing, the other students involved all thought it was hillarious including all the boys whom the other girls had inlisted, I still to this day cant be undresed around someone even my husband because I feel so embarresed.
- I am scared of Alchohol always have been bad experience when I was a young Child so one of the other girls in my year thought it would be funny to pretend that they had alchohol in there bag andf they were going to force me to drink it because they thought it would make me cooler even when I tried to get away from them the physically restrained me laughing about how funny it was to make me cry and then when the teacher came in they all thought it was a great joke because they got away with the act because it turned out that it was just a ginger beer bottle that looked like a beer stubbie
- Not one person spoke to me during year 11 in high school because I wasent one of the cool group and I stuck to my beliefs this only made it worse when my younger brother got sick and was thought

to be dying one of the girls in my class actually accused me of faking the whole thing just to get attention from people

12th December 2005

'I would love to be involved with your project it would be a healing experience for me man I could give you enough stories for a book just about me some of the other thing that have happened to me are:

- I walked into my year 10 formal and someone said OH my god it's a girl and they proceded to feel me up
- I was actually sexually assaulted by a fellow class mate and then was called a liar and a slut for a year
- Called vinnies because my clothes weren't always new
- Told that it is a good thing that my mother is blind (my mother has retinal dysraphy and is actually blind) because she cant see how ugly I am infront of a teacher and the teacher just laughed thinking it was hilarious even the tears
- I was told that I was faking a broken arm the day that it happened even though you could see the bone I was told by another student that I am an attention seeking bitch so I need to deal with the fact that it wasent my time in the spotlight
- Roumers were spread by an ex boyfriend that I has an insestuis relationship with my brother
- I was told to show up in Business clothes to a school excursion and when I did (in a smart suit) laughed at because everyone else was in jeans and a t shirt

13th December 2005

- In year 7 another students MOTHER came onto school grounds and belittled me because I was on the debaiting team and her daughter wasent and then processed to slap me across the face because I dared to stand up for myself . . . me that I am not worth spending time on because She was going to have my legs broken by someone IN front of staff members who did nothing once again
- I was raped by a class mate at the age of 15 and when I finally plucked up enough courage to tell someone about it all she did was laugh at me and say that he wouldn't touch me with a ten foot pole

because I was so ugly and . . . to go and tell my attacker what I had said my parents still made me go to school even after this when he then physically assaulted me in the toilets in order for me to keep my mouth shut and I didn't remember the incident again until . . . with my husband for the first time and I gave him a black eye I was so scared not good this is something I actually blocked out for 3 years as a result of my tortuous schooling

- On my leg there is a rather large birth mark and for 13 years of schooling I had to deal with every summer people telling me it was actually poo that was in some way god knows how where I used to wipe my backside when I went . . . probly don't have to tell you but it is physically impossible when the mark is on your knee

- Every day because my parents could not always afford to buy a lot of food I would have to bring a smaller portion of food than other students so they started a roumer that I had actually been kicked out of home for doing someth . . . of things out of other Students bins and they actually used to sit there and watch me eat and each person lay claim to whatever I was eating to this day I find it extremely uncomfortable to eat in public I normally can eat in public bu . . . getting better thanks to my husband and parents

- My mother as I told you is blind and I was told that I should be happy that she was blind because it meant that she couldn't see what a disappointment I must be to her because I was so ugly and had no boobs and I also love to . . . and that I am a compulsive liar

- At my year 12 graduation I was physically ill because I didn't want to deal with the crap for even that last night because I seemed to have finally gotten some peace in my life they actually booed me when I got up to accept my h . . . enough for people to complain about it but just enough for me to hear as I was going up the stairs there were only 4 people in my graduating class so imaging how that felt

- when you enter year 11 you are allowed to where make up so I thought I would BIG mistake one of the other girls in my class actually crashtackled me and stole my lipstick and then proceeded to smear it all over my face and j . . . because she tought it would be funny to see me look like an idiot even today I hardly ever where make up ony to weddings and funerals because of that experience

- I was sourt of friends with a teacher he was helping me with my public speaking for something so another student stared a roumer that we were having sex in the science lab at lunch everyday that's what we were really doing th . . . had to leave the school because of those roumers
- This is a great one told by the Principle of my school that I was not smart enough to do Chemistry or General English for my HSC in front of my parents I went into the school when I got my HSC results and had passed General . . . Refused to let me do Chemistry and showed him how smart I really am.

15th December, 2005

- when I was in year 12 they actually tied to arrange the year 12 formal without me knowing so I couldn't go the only reason I even knew it was on was because a teacher told me there were only 4 people in my whole class . . . really good
- When I had a crush on a boy for the first time I told one of my "FRIENDS" so she went and told him so they played a joke on my saying that he liked me to and that he wanted to go out with me then I got told by a teacher . . . joke does wonders for your mind at 14 years old
- Told that my parents didnt love me the only reason that they kept me around was because no one else would have me and they felt sorry for me and I was adopted from apes unfortunitly for them I look to much like my sib . . . adopted
- had another Student threaten to kill me because I refused to finsh of some work without her in a class so she could go of and have a cigarette that was fun
- everyone laughed when I had a gas bottle almost blow up in my face and told that no one would miss me even if I was killed
- They all tried to leave me on a school excursion into "******" because they thought it would be funny if a teacher hadn't noticed I was missing from the group I would have been forgotten.
- Had my lunch stolen many times ferom ym bag and later on it was heminite hygeen products when they knew they were there that was a great help let me assure you when I was bleeding heavily and couldn't do anything at . . . me Pads were gone.

8th July, 2006

'When I got my first boyfriend at school he wasent exactly the cutest boy out there but he had a heart of gold, anyway I remember one of the girls in my class, coming up to us and saying things to my boyfriend like Oh I saw "******" Kissing another boy, did you know that she is only going out with you because she feels so sorry for you because your so ugly. It took me a week to get him to speak to me again we continued to go out for 2 years but the relentlessness of the torture that this one girl put us both through took its tole on the both of us, at one point he had a collapsed lung and was in hospital when this girl came up to me at school and told me that I was so bad that he had to die to get away from me, He didn't die at all but at still really stressed me out let me assure you.

'One thing also is that the staff members at my school were all fully aware of what was going on and did nothing, even at times laughing at what students were taunting me with, oh what I wouldn't give to be able to sue some of those people now. Someone asked me the other day why am I not sending my kids to the school that I went to and my answer was plain and simple. I am not going to put my kids into a place where bullying is ignored and staff even take place in the torture. I have already decided that if my kids are going to be tortured the way I was in school I would rather home school them that them go through anything like what I went through.

17th July, 2006

'I was just talking to a friend from school who was helping me remember some more stories from school, on one occasion the girls in my class took my socks, shoes, school jumper and even my school skirt, leaving me stuck . . . oval, covering my bra thankfully no one else was able to see me, and myself and my best friends were late to class we were the ones who got detention for being late. When my friend stuck up for me during the times when people were picking on me and SHE was the one that other students parents tried to get expelled for being a bully, when she was the one trying to protect me.

'My 13 year old cousin "****" is going through hell at school being bullied she has had some awful things said to her and done to her, recently a boy spat in "****" face and when she slaped him across the face it was her who got so . . . was done to this boy how unfair is that "*******", "***" is overeating to try and get over the pain of being picked on and we have actually had to stage like an intervention to try and get her to open up to all of us about whats going on si . . . that she shouldn't have been born and that she would be better of dead also her Mother had a stroke and some idioc child told her that her mother needs to be put down and out of her misery.

'I am actually going to go to "*******" School tomorrow and talk to them about maybe doing a bullying seminar at the school for the girls in Year 8 and 9, because they are the problem they need to hear some of the horror stories . . .;

26th September, 2006

'I have something interesting to share with you a so called friend of mine and I were talking the other day about how School has affected us in later life and she was saying how hard done by she is because she is a reformed drug addict and has issues with her parents, and how I had it so easy in my life and I have no right to complain about the bullying she and I both endured during school, from both students and teachers, YES teachers even bullied me, (will share more on that in a minute) and continued to tell me how people hated her because she was my friend and she wish she had never layed eyes on me and all this horrendis stuff, in the end I threw her out of my house and told her she was not welcome here ever again and then she actually turned around and said that it was her who iniciated the bullying I endured during school because she was so resentful of the fact that even though I had it tough growing up I always had the love of my parents even during the tough times with them, and they supported me no matter what, apparently her parents thought I was the greatest thing since sliced bread and told her constantly that she should be more liked me, so she decided to take revenge on me by making my life outside the home a living hell, this all took place on my front lawn, I cant tell you how floored I was at this, but I can tell you now it sure explains how the people doing the picking always knew private things about me I never even thought that this person would betray me in such a way, it really in increadible what lengths people will go to for revenge against someone.

'Anyway just a quick story about an instint with a teacher, I was in year 11 Ancient history and we were studing ancient Rome and of cource with a name like "******" I was the contant butt of jokes and many idiotic things said by class mates with a surname like "******" it has got to be expected but when the teacher joins in with the teasing that's going to far, we were studing "****** ******s" death and teacher proceeded to ask if it hurt to be stabbed to death aimed at me and he keep going asking me stupid things like what was it like to now be a girl, I went to the principle about it and nothing was ever done, because no one in my class every supported my story they all decided early on that I was not going to be supported.'

CASE TWENTY FOUR

(Written in 2005)

'I am an 18 year old girl from a town in "Hungerford", and from the ages of about 7 until I left high school in year ten I was bullied by not only girls, but boys too. I guess they saw me as an easy target because I was always lacking confidence in myself and always wanted approval. In primary school I had about 5 friends who always excluded me from the group whenever they wanted, they would talk about me behind my back and spred rumours about me throughout school. Even the boys would come up to me and say "your so ugly", "you've only got small boobs, all the other girls boobs are big" and "big nose". Yes they are really harsh and hurtful things but I didn't care what they said because I was the girls that were my sometimes friends were my only friends.

'We all then went to the same high school and of course the same thing happened there but worse because there were more people. I made enemies straight away but I didn't understand why no one liked me, all through year eight I got bashed about 3 times a week. I have been hit over the head with text books, continuously had a basketball slammed into my head and even had a tomato squashed into my face. All by the same girl but rallied on by all her mates. I never stood up to her, I just took it. I honestly wanted to die and in ten ten I did try to kill myself. I slit my rists but nothing happened. I just thought I was even more of a failure because I couldn't enev manage to kill myself.

'Anyway, my bully left at year eight but her friends just bullied me while she was away. I was always in the sick bay trying to avoid them. I took out an A.V.O against my bully but that didn't matter because in year nine she came back and the school put her in all of my classes. So another year of getting hit, being called a slut, and living in absolute fear. In year

78

ten it was the same again. But only one thing changed, one bully became two bullies. The first one was the same build as me, which is small, and the second bully was huge. Towards the end of the year I was really getting fed up with all the shit that I had gone through. One day the big bully was all up in my face yelling at me, saying something about I had said something bad about one of her friends and now I'm going to pay for it.

'She had me by the front of my shirt and my feet were literally off the ground. She had her fist in the air ready to punch me, I was scared shitless. But through my fear I somehow managed to be confident and stand up to her. She was saying she was going to smash me and I replied in a really sarcastic but yet overpowering tone "So are you gonna hit me yet or what?". She put me down and said sternly "No, but that was a warning". That was the last time I have ever been bullied. I still see both of those girls every so often and they say hello and ask how I am. I can't believe after all those years I was bullied all it took for them to leave me alone was to stand up to them and really mean it. Almost four years on I can see that they only picked on me not because of who I was as a person but because they knew that I would take it. Well I did and I won't anymore. I have also found out numerous things about myself. I am smart, intelligent, damn attractive with a fine body and that no matter what I thought before, I am loved. I have an amazing partner who always manages to make me feel like a princess, I have a great career that many people would love to have and everything I have, I bought all by myself. When you are being bullied you never imagine you could ever be happy but am really happy with the way things turned out for me and I am extremely content with life. And the one thing I thought I would never be; I am confident.

'So if there is a message I can say to people being bullied, "You are loved, be confident, stand up for yourself, don't take any shit from anyone, and truly be who you really are not who people think you should be."

CASE TWENTY FIVE

(Written in 2005)

'My son his name is "John" was born with a muscle deficiency and arthritis so we tended to protect him a lot thus rendering him reliant on us and insecure this is the thing the bullies draw on I found anyway.

'"John" was in grade 1 when it started he was being bullied by a grade 6 can you believe it.

'but what I found out was this child was being bullied by his peers, He forever punched and hit my son.

'he was receiving red cards to bring home this meant his parents had to sign to acknowledge that he had been in trouble.

'but this didn't stop it got to the point I used to have to go to school to check up on him. "John" is a very quiet child he would report it to teachers but told to go find someone else to play not thinking this kid used to seek him out

'it was torment for 2 terms it only stopped 1—cos I rang the parents and had a meeting with them and the principle and 2—cos the child ended up dying in an accident so I will never know if the meeting truly worked.'

CASE TWENTY SIX

(Written in 2005)

'The following case is written by two people . . . the victim's personal record of her own experience, and the second is written from the viewpoint of her mother. Again names have been changed to protect the innocent.

'I am 13 years old and am in Grade 7. I have been bullied for most of my school life. None of the kids at school want me to be in their group, except for my 4 friends, who all get picked on as well. My friend "Jane" gets teased because she is overweight. My friend "Ali" gets teased because of the street that she lives in. "Anne" gets teased because of her pimples, the street that she lives in and they just don't like her. In Primary School people used to say that I pick my nose and eat it because one boy said that I did and spread it around the whole school. Even in High School now, one older kid who didn't know me asked me if I picked my nose. When I was in Primary School I was usually last or second last to be picked as a partner or for a group. This made me feel embarrassed and left out. People used to moan because they had to have me in their group. I don't know why people are so mean to me because I am always nice to them. One time I let a boy borrow my things and I heard him say sucker behind my back. The only time boys ever really talk to me is when they want to borrow something. I have told the teacher a couple of times when something bad has happened to me but there isn't much they can do about it. People never liked me touching them as they said that I had germs and they would try to pass the germs onto their friends when they touched me. One time some older kids threw a bottle that hit me in the head and laughed about it. Everywhere I used to go I got "accidentally" hit in the head with balls and things. A boy in my class always throws paper and tape at me, and everybody laughs. No-one will sit close to me in class. All of the boys moan if they are forced to sit next to me in class. This makes me feel left out and embarrassed too.

'I wish people would just be nice to me and treat me like they do other people. I don't think people like me because I'm different, because I'm nice to people. I would like to try and help people who get bullied. I hate how people treat other people that have problems like ADHD. People who get teased the same as me, or are different, seem to like me more than the popular people do.'

And the same story, as told by the mother of the victim.

'"Melanie" is now 13 years old, and in Grade 7 at High School. All of her school life she has been bullied, never physically, but more by exclusion. I cannot understand why, as she is quite attractive, not overweight, very polite and is just a little shy around crowds of people. She has been fortunate enough through school to always have one good friend, which certainly helps her to cope. The exclusion that she faces every day is absolutely heartbreaking. Nobody, except a couple of friends, talks to her and everybody whispers things about her. Her classmates always "borrow her things" and either don't return them or don't bother to say thanks. Everything she says during group work is ignored or discounted. She is one of the last children to be picked for school sports and team work activities. She has been to three different schools, and it has occurred in all of them. This has led to her having low self esteem and she suffers from anxiety. Because it has been going on for so long, she is very accepting of the fact that "everybody at school hates me". I always ensure that she wears the same clothes as everybody else and do everything I can to make her "fit in", but nothing works. She is an only child, but has always had plenty of opportunities to mix with kids from the time she was 18 months old, through Day Care and various playgroups, so I was shocked when she was bullied from the time she started school. She is a very giving/forgiving girl so has had various friends over the years that have taken advantage of her good nature and "used" her when there is no-one else to hang around with. I have approached all of the schools that she has attended with my concerns, but, as it is not physical bullying, there is nothing that seems to work. All of the schools have had anti-bullying policies and talks to the children, but nothing seems to make any difference. Both "Melanie" and I have to live with the devastating effects that this bullying has. "Melanie" has been to counselling, but does not "open up" easily to strangers and refuses to go again, and I am at my wits end to know what to do. I find it the saddest thing when she says "nobody likes me but I don't care anymore, I'm used to it". What a devastating statement for a child to make. Children can certainly be cruel. The only positive to come out of this is that "Melanie" has a real sense of compassion for others, particularly the underdog and will help those in need. If someone is crying in the playground, she will be the first one there to offer comfort and help. She has an understanding (sadly) of how cruel a place the world can be and subsequently wants to make it a better place for all, and I'm sure she will.

'I have no answers to the problem of bullying and how to stop it, but hope that all schools will continue to look at ways of dealing with the problem, as I know first hand the devastating effects it has on kids.'

CASE TWENTY SEVEN

(Written in 2005)

'To whom it may concern,

'Im writing with regards to bullying. I was bullied from year 2 through to the end of year 6 by one particular girl. She would spit on me,push me, call me a retard,spastic because a have 2 severley disabled brothers. When it was happening I didnt cry in front of her as I didnt want her to have the satisfaction. I would run to the toilets with my best friend and cry. The problem was that this girl didnt understand that just because my brothers were disabled didnt mean that I was. I learnt to ignore this girl with the encouragement of my family and friends, I knew that yelling at her or pushing her back would only bring me to her level. I actually felt sorry for her as she didnt relise just how special people are that have disabilitys. I think parents need to be more open with there kids about disabilitys rather than treating them as aliens. the good thin for me was that this girl ended up at the same high school as me, In year seven I recieved a card from her to say sorry for all that she had done to me for 4 years. I didnt hold any grudges and accepted the apology, I thought that was very brave of her as she had been very nasty. We spent the rest of our years at the same school being friends. Sometimes you can have a nice ending to bullying'.

Another story from the same victim:

'I also was bullied by my teacher during year 5 and 6. Unfortunately I had her both years. It started out in year 5 when I approached her about the bullying I was receiving from that girl. She told me to stop lying. After that she saw me as an easy target and told me to stop using my brothers disabilitys as an excuse. I was locked in our storeroom during class several times. I was also made to sit under our blackboard in the classroom while everyone had the class christmas party. I wasnt allowed to turn around and look. Unfortunatley I did and was locked in the storeroom.

'The reasons why she did this were petty. One of them being that we had a journal book that we wrote down things that we were doing on the weekend and write our thoughts. I wrote how I was playing softball and that my coach was a poo. I wrote this as our coach expected too much from our team sometimes.

'My teacher saw what I wrote, she took me to the incinerater and burnt my book and locked me in the storeroom. My mum approached the school about this, but they wernt much help. In year 6 it got worse she would pick on me and blame me for things I didnt do. Always reminding me not to use my brothers disabilitys as an excuse. I still suffer from low self confidence every now and then, I have 18 month old twins and will be on the alert when they are old enough to attend school. I will not tolerate them bullying people and I will teach them to be open with me if they are being bullied so that we can combat it together without bullying back.'

CASE TWENTY EIGHT

'As a child when I first started school, I was treated something terrible by other children, me being poor and because my mum had to work for this girls mother, they were just plain "snobs", there were about eight girls in this group, "Jennifer" being the leader. They would wait till I came down to the toilets They would get me & push my head in the toilet. They were pans then at the bottom of the school Grounds, they would chase me all around the Play Ground, I was a terribly shy Person or child, one day my Cousin "Tania" saw them, what they were doing, She was crippled, curviture of the spine, She went mad at them & said, "leave my cousin alone", They pushed her over, it was hard for "Tania" to get up, one had to stand on her feet and pull her up, which I had to do, "Tania" was a bit older than me in a higher class, she was a beautiful person never complained about her pain, when I look back I think now she was a angel, I used to pass her place on the way to school so we often went together, she used to call me, "*****", came from spirit once. They The mediam said "***** was called from a distant", I know she would be with the Angels of the higher light. I was very sad when she died at twelve years of age, she ended up in a wheel chair, then I went to see her when she was bed ridden not long before she died. One day the kids were chasing me as mum had bought me a brand new mug. "Jennifer" had one the same. I didn't know this, she accused me of stealing hers, they chased me all over the playground, "Tania" intervened & told them she was going to report them, as she told them I was no thief, We were all called up to the class room, The teacher told "Jennifer" to look in her bag in the desk, yes her mug was there, The teacher really went mad at her & the others, they were warned about ever hurting me again, her friends were not happy with her any more, so after that things settled down. But that stayed with me the rest of my life, I was only five & six years old then, At "Jennifer's" mothers house where mum worked, we lived there in a couple of rooms up in the back paddock, it was full of mice, they would nible at my hair at night, I used to help mum with all the dishes at night, sometimes till eleven o'clock at night, Mum had a lot of people to cook for it as it was a big boarding place, "Jennifer" one day I was sitting out on the great big lawn out the front, she went mad at me & told me to get around the back, where I belonged, I walked around the back, then their ginger cat sprang out & scratched me on the leg. The humilliation those snobs of people caused me. then when I went to the biger school, it happened again, there was this girl by the name of "Edwards", who would follow me home & kick & hit me in the head she was like a Tom boy, this night I was that hurt I was crying pretty bad, when "Wendy", my sister, wanted to know why I was crying, as I do not remember telling mum or my sisters before. So "Wendy" said she would be watching after school, so she was waiting down in the paddock, & saw what was happening, she made me fight this girl, I still held back, but this girl hit me in the face & next before I realised I punched her right in the nose & made it bleed. She ran home screaming, she never touched me again.

'Then we moved to "Rockville" later on, I made many friends at "hampton" school. My friend went through humilliation from the teacher, she used to pick on her all the time, I sat in the same seat as "Rose Parker". we had the old ink pens then. She used to hit "Rose" on the back & make her put ink all over the page, She told me to take her to the head masters & show him what she had done to her work. I took her to the Office, but I told "Mr Smith" exactly what happened, he told us to wait there, later he came back, he said we could go back to the class room, when we got there we had a new teacher. Things were okay after that, we never saw that teacher again. I guess all these things are lessons through life that we have to learn to make us stronger and we can only do the best we can and always try to keep that love and strengh as when I was married, I was again put down and surpresed for many years to come, I am glad that part of my life is over, as I live a more peaceful life now, I try not take in the negitive and try to keep the positive, as negitive is a terrible drain on one's energy, and can make one sick. in meditation I find I am nearest to God and the beauty around. Peace is within the heart and love will have more power than anything else on earth.

'Having been very sick as a new born baby, they say one can develop low Self Esteem, I neary went back to Spirit mum said, when I was four days old. Mum said my Auntie dropped me on my head when I was a Baby, I wonder if that is when I got the curvature in the neck or when he stamped on my head when "Tom" was four years old, I lost my memory for three days, then I also had whiplash a couple of times, I was very shy from a young child, I was very vulnerable as I got older, I now know he saw this in me, I feel like I never had a chance to overcome my problems, until years later. When I came in contact with aggressive people or self centr'd people or those who put people down or one that do not care about others feelings, who do not give of them selves, these things used to worry me and hold me back, I was often in the middle of these people but then I realize we are all here to learn lessons To make us stronger, we are not suppose to judge.'

CASE TWENTY NINE

(Written in 2007)

The following is more a comment and advice, rather than the experience itself, written by the victim:

'I am 24 now but have had a streak of bullying from back in the grade 7 until the later years, almost graduating years of high school. Though I am not suffering from bullies anymore much due to self help and retaining a different outlook on life when I took to trying to help other people who were going through bullying like I did, it still has a inlasting impression of a life that was very depressing back then. My personal medicine is to talk about bullying with other people still in high school and I would love to someday write myself though have never had enough personal experience etc in the department. I would love for other people to be able to read about normal people of their age group going through a simular experience and being able to know that most people pull out of it and realize in the long run that they are the better person through experiencing the pain of bullying.

'I have learnt personally through that experience that in knowing the emotional toll this can have on a person I will never bully anyone and will go the step further to try and help any bullying I can in the future'.

CASE THIRTY

(Written in 2008)

'well my story is that i was bullied from the age of 13 upwards until i left school at 17, i had been picked on in primary school but nothing like what it became like when i went to high school(age 13).

'the weird thing is i had loads of friends but i still got teased and made fun of constantly, i was very different, i didnt want to be the same as everyone else, i was a bit punky, i had different hair and hair colour all the time, i customised all my clothes etc, I'm still like that but things are very different now.

'my dream was to become a nurse(which i have achieved) so as a result i had to study hard so i got picked on for that too, i was a bit overweight too so that didnt help matters and i got called ugly all the time and boys made fun of me and made gagging faces to describe me . . . as i said i had plenty of friends and they tried to stick up for me but it didnt really work, i wasnt like everyone else because my parents are quite strict so i wasnt out partying and drinking like alot of people my age, when i think about it now i didn't really stand a chance!

'the one thing that saved me from complete meltdown was my friends and my music, i can sing and play several instruments and was involved in bands and musical theatre so i got some respect through that.

'i think the worst thing for me was when this girl that i barely knew started bullying me and she has to a certain extent kept it up to this day even though we are now both adults and have moved on with our lives, she is now a mother of two, i have moved to another country and have made a great life for myself, this girl i had never spoken two words to in my life and she suddenly decided that she should take the piss(excuse the language) of me for what ever reasons in my last year at school, saying my name mockenly etc, anyway as i mentioned before, i moved to another country to go to university and become a nurse, i grew up, i lost weight, i became a bit more worldly and i have a fantastic life. this particular girl is a nightmare, more than once i've been home. and she has made some smart arse comment after all these years, i can hand on heart say that i have forgiven the people in school who bullyed me because we were all young and foolish and i don't want to go around the rest of my life and hold grudges against dozens of people but this girl is a different story, i know that it is her own insecurity that she feels like she has to bring other people down but it still hurts, i ignore her but i have a lot of angry feelings towards her, mainly because i feel i should have left all that behind me a long time ago, i do believe it is her problem not mine and i move on with my life and ignore her if she tries to wind me up.

'anyway the moral of my story is that (excuse the cheesiness) is that i have come through bullying and I am a very strong(if maybe a bit wary), independent person who in all honesty has a fantastic life, i have achieved my dream of becoming a nurse, i have travelled and i have lovely friends who love me, i rarely feel like i dont fit in anymore even though I'm still a bit punky and different!!! every now and again the bullying comes back to haunt me but all i can do is try every day not to let it get me down or effect my relationships with people(because it sometimes does) or my confidence (which it probably does quite a bit) i have forgiven those people who were unkind because as i said we all do things we regret when we are young and as for that other girl who insists of keeping the whole thing going well I just have to ignore her and get on with my life . . .'

CASE THIRTY ONE

'When I was younger & leaving home to go to school, I always felt like I was going to be sick, butterflies in tummy etc. When I arrived to the skl yard I would notice my group running to hide from me. Did they think I was stupid & not see, NOT ME. This happened for at least a year on/off, plus other guys or girls laughing at me now & again. Then it was time to start H/skl. Well, new friends, new beginnings, but I still kept some of my old friends. But once we started H/SKL everyone moved on & met new people, so did I. then the bullying started again, but a lot worse. This time one girl in the group would do votes wit other girls in group to see who wanted me or not. Of course the highest votes was for me to leave the group. I used to hate it. I did have all diff types of friends so Iwasn't totally alone. Lunch times would hang out in library, to kill time.

'When Yr 10 was ova I was out of there, to start a new life, and indeed I did. Going to the school's renunions never have interested me, & some girls that used to bully me have seen them shopping, & they are so nice, but to me I really don't think much of them at all!'

CASE THIRTY TWO

(Written in 2005)

'I was 14 years old and second year of high school. The first year was good and I hung out with a group of girls. Finding I was getting into too much trouble I decided to break away from them and concentrate on my schooling.

'Things went along well until the girls decided to take a bit of revenge on me. It wasn't the right thing to do breaking away from them or so they thought. They started tormenting me and threatening me. I thought I would do the right thing and went to one of the teachers and told her about it. Needless to say she spoke to the people involved then the real fun began. Every corner I went around they seemed to be there and mouthing off at me. They would take every opportunity to bump into me but would put their fist in first.

'One day the class had swimming and we all went to the pools. The girls that were onto me managed to hold me back when it was time to go back to class and they cornered me. There were about six girls and they grabbed me and tried to push me into the pool. It took them a while I put up a great fight but six onto one was too much and in I went, clothes and all. They all stood and laughed then left. I got out of the pool and went home.

'My mother was horrified and marched me back to school and got the principal involved. As it turned out I wasn't the only one getting bullied. He told my mother I was the third that had reported this sort of thing. He spoke to the girls involved and they were suspended from school for a time. After that time and they were due back at school things got scary.

'My schoolwork started to go down and so did I. I was too scared to go to school. I'd make any excuse to stay home until I just couldn't bring myself to getting out of bed. My mother thought I had some sort of virus and kept me there. She called the Dr and he ran a lot of tests but nothing showed up. I had no idea what was wrong only that I had no energy to do anything.

'At the time I had a boyfriend and he came into see me one lunchtime. I told him then that I wanted to end my life, it wasn't worth living anymore. He told me he loved me and if I did that then it would mean I didn't love him. I was so in love with him but couldn't find any other way of stopping the feelings I was feeling and thought that was the only way I would be able to stop the helplessness. I just wanted to die to get away from it all.

'My mother told me she was going to the shop and that was when I went into the bathroom and grabbed any pill I could find and take them. Then I went into my sister's room and found a scalpel. She used to make sheepskin slippers and would use the scalpel to cut the sheepskin. I put the scalpel to my wrist and cut. The blood ran and I felt scared but relieved at the same time. The pills started to take effect and I felt sleepy so I went back to bed and went to sleep.

'The next thing I remembered was Mum sitting on the bed talking to me. I started to cry and put my hand up to wipe the tears. Mum saw the cuts and rushed to phone the Dr. I was put into the psychiatric ward at the hospital and had a lot of counseling.

'I'm now 46 years old. I have been married twice and have five children. My second husband and I moved to Australia from another nation 4 years ago.

'I spent a good part of my life on anti-depressants and now my youngest daughter is going through something very similar. She is the same age that I was and I know if I don't react to this right away it will ruin her life like it did mine. I feel for her and know exactly what she is going through.

'I hope the bullies out there that may read your book can get some insight on what they can do to a persons life and the impact it had to the those they are bullying.'

CASE THIRTY THREE

(Written in 2007)

'For many years in primary school I was teased. I was always called a teachers pet because I got good grades and spent most of my time reading or on computers. There were other names but it was the physical abuse that scarred me mentally. The physical abuse started in 4th grade when I dared to tell a bully to bugger off and leave me alone . . . HE then king hit me on the arm, leaving a bruise that lasted over 3 months (he took martial arts lessons and knew full well what he was doing . . .). Later in that same year I was beaten severely by two 6th graders for taking my shoe off to check a wound of all things. I ended up with facial swelling and bruising and a concussion. What astonishes me is the lack of caring from the teachers. I sat in sick bay from lunchtime til 2:45 pm (15mins before school ended mind you) when they decided they would call my mother to come and get me. I was taken to hospital as I had blurry vision and a killer headache. The girls received a detention. My mother decided to call the police and the girls were given a stern warning and the school was made to pay for my hospital fees (xrays, painkillers and follow up visits) . . . After this incident, I left and was home schooled for 18months . . .

'As if that incident wasn't enough to scare and scar any child, when I reached high school 3yrs later (I was made to repeat year 6 when I went back to school—apparently my social skills weren't up to scratch) . . . the bullying started almost immediately. I originally got called names or pushed over and jostled by the peers I was MEANT to go up from year 6 with however the bullying although demeaning, wasnt severe. Later in my first semester, some (5) older girls (year 10)were taunting me as I walked to the bathrooms. I chose to ignore them but that wasnt the response they were after it seems . . . They followed me and about halfway across the

playground one of them grabbed my shirt and basically had a go at me
for not responding to their taunts. I simply shrugged her off and told her
there was no point in me responding and continued to the bathroom. She
the grabbed my shirt again and another girl grabbed the front of me and
they started shoving me so I told them quite bluntly to piss off and leave
me alone. Thats when they physically belted the living crap out of me. I
remember defending off a couple of initial blows and getting one of my
own in before I saw a fist aimed right at my temple. When I came to a
couple of minutes later they were kicking my back, neck and stomach. The
teacher FINALLY notices (how observant . . . you would think the crowd
of students yelling "fight fight fight" would alert them to a violent situation
in their playground but I guess not) and breaks up the fight (or rather
belting as it turned out to be). He then had 4 students help me to the sick
bay. I was bleeding from the mouth and nose, my vision was blurry and
my back, ribs, kidneys and stomach hurt like hell, not to mention the killer
headache I had. The principal, rather than seeking the medical attention
I clearly needed, decided it was much more appropriate for me to fill out
incident report forms detailing what had just occurred and then made me
relay the story over and over and over again. I started to feel really sleepy
and dizzy so he gave me an ice pack and told me to lay down. I did . . . and
promptly threw up. He said I would be ok and that he was going to call my
mother. This was at approx. 12:30pm I'm told . . . my mother got to the
school at 2:30pm and said that he had rung her just after 1:30pm and boy
was she mad when she saw what state I was in. She abused him like nothin
else. By now bruises and swelling on my body was occurring and I was still
groggy and dizzy and nauseous and sore so mum took me straight to the
hospital, telling the principal she would deal with him later. As it turns
out, I had a fractured check, fractured eye socket, 2 broken ribs, a bruised
spleen, bruised kidneys, brusing of the spine and a severe concussion. Now
I get cluster headaches and migraines on and off and I have a hump on my
neck . . . I am told both are a result of that beating . . .

    'Mum went back to the school the next day asking why the girls parents
werent called and why werent the girls being punished and he simply said
"I didn't think it was necessary"—Mum wasnt impressed, particularly when
he told her that all 5 girls were stating that I had started the fight with them
and mum pointed out that why would a lone 7th grader pick a fight with
5 10th graders for one and that for two, I had never been a violent person.
He said majority ruled in their favour and I was given AN IN SCHOOL
SUSPENSION . . . I was PUNISHED for being the VICTIM! We called

the police, the girls were warned and that was the end of it. Being 15 the police said that the girls were "too young" to be charged . . . I now know thats a load of BULL and wish I could have had them charged . . .

'I stayed on at school (after 4 weeks of healing and recuperating and trying to psych myself into going back to school) and thought that would be the end of it . . . Not so. The principal had apparently spoken to the girls, informing them of my injuries and then apparently gave them a lecture on physical abuse and told them to leave me be. I wish he hadnt done that. The girls started to follow me into the toilets. One day not long after returning, they locked me in there with them and started taunting me about the injuries they had caused, feeling rather proud of themselves. I told them just to leave me alone and tried to push past them. I ended up with a broken nose and a busted lip. I went to the principal and he called the girls in . . . they said I had shoved one of them and it was in self defence. I ended up on a stricter in school suspension. This happened a couple of times . . . they didnt always physically abuse me but they always shoved me and taunted me. I left in August that year and never went back to any high school—I was so scared and scarred that I decided to wait until I turned 15 and enrolled in TAFE.

'I was APPALLED at the actions of not only the girls but teachers, students and the principal in these situations, particularly the last one. No one gave a damn and no one ever came to my aid until it was far too late. I have permanent mental scarring and permanent physical problems due to that last severe beating and there is nothing that can be done about it anymore. I fear seeing any of the girls involved in the last beating in town as they do still harass me. They will deliberately throw their shoulder into me or trip me over in the shops if they see me, so if I see them I tend to panic and go in the complete opposite direction.

'That is my story . . . its not exactly a pretty one but thats what happened to me in school and I know I WILL NEVER allow any of my children to suffer that extent of bullying. Name calling and a little bit of pushing I feel is part of growing up but when it turns to constant harassment and physical abuse, something needs to be done. I know I will make sure the school and police act appropriately should one of my children ever be bullied severely, and if they don't, my child will be removed from that school.'

CASE THIRTY FOUR

(Written in 2010)

This victim had immense problems writing his experiences down and after several attempts, sadly had to give up. But what he was able to get down is as follows:

'I am 48yo I lost sight in one eye 30 years ago but that did not stop me from completing my apprenticeship and becoming a talented tradesman then running a successful business employing other people. When the drought hit our region 10 years ago business slowed down so I shut up shop and moved my family to another state. I applied for a job and told my employer I was blind in 1 eye before he gave me the job. The conditions we worked in where very harsh and I didnt think I would last long but I stuck to it and after about a year was given a good pay rise while others missed out. I could understand why tradesman's can sometimes only last a few days or hours working in those conditions. I went and seen a GP for something minor when he noticed a red spot in my good eye.

Continued in a different email, from the same victim:

'The GP told me to see a eye specialist, he told me I had sun cancer in my only eye and it could be fixed with a 1 night stay in hospital but would need time off work so my eye could be covered to recover from the op.

And from another email:

'After the op I went back to work but my eye was still sore and blood red after 3 months I rang the surgeon he said it should be better by now and needed to have another look. He gave me the bad news that I needed another op and I started to get worried about my family future.

And a final email, before he was forced to give up:

'So I booked in to get surgrey and booked some unpaid time off, 2 days before I was to stop work again we had a very hard night and I left a seal pick on a machine (looks like a dentist hook tool) The next change over shift a worker said he found this pick and wanted to know how owned it, 1 off the blokes said I am sure that belongs to "Andy". In front of everyone and me not being present the supervisor said I should pick his . . .'

CASE THIRTY FIVE

(Written in 2007)

'As a child I was bullied for 5yrs in primary school. The main reason I feel I was bullied was because I lived in a caravan park and was often refered to as a gypsy and a lot of the kids weren't allowed to play with me for that reason so I wonder if the main cause was the parents. I was bullied on a daily basis and as a result I spent most of my time alone and even to this day it upsets me and if I see these same people today I'm still intimidated by them. By the time I had reached high school, we were living in a house so the problem didn't exist as much. I was also bullied by a teacher and now as an adult I realize what he did had a sexual nature because he pulled my pants down and spanked my bare butt for no apparent reason and then sent me down to kindergarten even though I was in 3rd class. I do know my father sent a letter of protest to him but I've no idea what he said and I can't remember if I told my parents about the spanking'.

CASE THIRTY SIX

(Written in 2010)

'I have 2 short stories as i was bullied from the age of 10 right through to the end off High School. It still happens on occasion but i am better equipped in dealing with it now.

'When i was 10 we had to get up in class and tell where we were from. Our school was a mixture of say 70% Australian 30% ethnic background. So when it came to my turn i stood up and told the class that my parents were from another nation. It would have been maybe a week later that i was confronted by some of the students from my class and called a ****. I went home that afternoon and asked my mother what a **** was. She asked me why I was asking I explained to her what we had to do in class and she was not very happy. I know she went to the Headmaster and complained to him. I can only presume my 5th class teacher got into trouble as she treated me differently from then on so much so that i failed 5th class my report that year was the worst I'd ever had. The taunts didn't stop from the students either. Some of the boys who lived near me used to ride their push bikes past my house yelling out **** go home. That would have been a bit hard for me as I was born here in Australia.

'In High school the racial taunts stopped. I went to an all girls school and in the 80's there were a lot of Vietnamese people moving into the area and coming to the school. They had someone else to pick on. But my so called group of friends there was 4 of us were the instigators this time. We were having lunch one day and i was eating some Sao biscuits. One of them grabbed them off me and rubbed them into my hair and face. Then they all started laughing and jumping and pointing at me loudly so other people then started looking at me. Another time they rubbed grapes into my hair. The end came when they talked another girl into kicking the bottom of my feet as I had them stretched in front of me. I asked this girl to stop numerous times but she didn't. I did retaliate and I am not proud of what I did I slapped this girl across the face. I ran away in tears first going to an empty class room then going to the mistress in charge of girls and told her what had happened and what I had done. She understood why I slapped the girl but explained that I shouldn't have done it. The others wire hauled into her office and told off. I was advised not to hang around these girls again advise I listened to and for the next 2 years had no problems at all.'

www.ingramcontent.com/pod-product-compliance
Lightning Source LLC
Chambersburg PA
CBHW030401290526
45785CB00004B/1858